Reiki Healing Touch

AND THE Way OF Jesus

BRUCE G. EPPERLY, PHD

KATHERINE GOULD EPPERLY, DMIN

Reiki Healing Touch

AND

THE Way

OF Jesus

Northstone

Editor: Michael Schwartzentruber
Cover and interior design: Margaret Kyle
Proofreading: Dianne Greenslade
Cover illustration: www.photos.com

Unless otherwise noted, all biblical quotations are from
the New Revised Standard Version, copyright 1989 by
the Division of Christian Education of the National Council of Churches of Christ
in the USA. All rights reserved. Used by permission.

NORTHSTONE PUBLISHING is an imprint of WOOD LAKE BOOKS INC. Wood Lake Books
acknowledges the financial support of the Government of Canada, through the Book Publishing
Industry Development Program (BPIDP) for its publishing activities.

WOOD LAKE BOOKS is an employee-owned company, committed to caring for the environment
and all creation. Wood Lake Books recycles, reuses, and encourages readers to do the same.
Resources are printed on recycled paper and more environmentally friendly groundwood papers
(newsprint), whenever possible. The trees used are replaced through donations to
the Scoutrees For Canada Program.
A percentage of all profit is donated to charitable organizations.

Library and Archives Canada Cataloguing in Publication
Epperly, Bruce Gordon
Reiki healing touch : and the way of Jesus/Bruce G. Epperly,
Katherine Gould Epperly.
Includes bibliographical references.
ISBN 1-896836-75-5
1. Reiki (Healing system) I. Gould Epperly, Katherine, 1950-
II. Title.
RZ403.R45E66 2005   616.8'52   C2005-904121-8

Published by Northstone Publishing
an imprint of WOOD LAKE BOOKS, INC.
9025 Jim Bailey Road, Kelowna, BC, Canada, V4V 1R2
250.766.2778
www.northstone.com
www.woodlakebooks.com

Printing 10 9 8 7 6 5 4 3 2 1
Printed in Canada
at Houghton Boston Printers, SK

CONTENTS

A WORD OF THANKS

Jesus' image of the vine and the branches reminds us of the profound interconnectedness of life in which we are constantly giving and receiving God's healing energy. This book is the result of our own interconnectedness manifest in the generosity of our reiki teachers – John Harvey Gray, Linda Kaiser, and Mary Jane Pagan. Each made reiki healing touch come alive and inspired us to share God's healing touch in our pastoral ministries, friendships, and family lives. All we can say is "thank you" for your insight and commitment to healing the earth one person at a time.

We are grateful to our families, especially to Maxine Gould, Kate's mother; and to Matt Epperly, our son, whose love and support has been constant. Bruce's father, the late Everett Epperly, taught him the importance of theological reflection in the art of ministry. We are grateful to our reiki and spiritual formation students throughout the United States and Canada. Bruce initially explored the interplay of reiki and Christianity with classes at Ghost Ranch Conference Center, New Mexico; Ring Lake Ranch, Wyoming; and Kirkridge Retreat and Study Center, Pennsylvania; and Naramata Centre, British Columbia. We give thanks to the participants who helped us with issues of connection and clarity. It is our prayer that this text and the integration of reiki and Christian faith will support God's passion to heal our world in this challenging time.

PROLOGUE

THE HORIZON OF HEALING

The true light, which enlightens everyone, was coming into the world.

John 1:9

You are the light of the world. A city built on a hill cannot be hid. No one after lighting a lamp puts it under the bushel basket, but on the lampstand, and it gives light to all in the house. In the same way, let your light shine before others, so that they may see your good works, and give glory to your [Parent] in heaven.

Matthew 5:14–16

Following one of Jesus' healings, the astonished crowd murmured, "We have seen strange things today" (Luke 5:26). As we look at the horizons of healing in the 21st century, we are also seeing strange things. The wall of separation erected nearly five centuries ago by the powers of science and religion in order to preserve their respective territories is now crumbling. Physicians are studying the sacred, and ministers and laypersons inside and outside the churches are claiming spirituality as an essential component in the healing process.

To the question, "Is religion good for your health?" a growing consensus in the medical community is responding with a unequivocal, "Yes." Medical studies suggest that regular attendance in worship and faithful commitment to the spiritual disciplines of prayer and meditation are significant factors in longevity, positive aging, coping with serious illness, minimizing the risks of high blood pressure and cardiovascular disease, reducing substance abuse, and decreasing stress-related illness.[1] Studies that indicated the positive impact of intercessory prayer in recovery from heart surgery inspired one physician to proclaim, "prayer is good medicine."[2] Medical schools now offer courses in spirituality and medicine, as well as in physician self-care. Theologians and spiritual directors teach physicians, psychiatric residents, and medical students how to deepen their spiritual lives through meditative prayer, while instructing them in the vital relationship between religion and mental health.

Medical surveys indicate the growing impact of complementary and alternative medical practices in the prevention of and response to disease. Along with Western medical treatments, many North Americans respond to health problems by using acupuncture, T'ai Chi, and Qi Gong from China; Ayurvedic medicine and yoga from India; and homeopathic, chiropractic, and herbal medicine from the United States and Europe.[3] Others explore the healing practices of Native American and African spiritual guides and medicine persons. Traditional religious practices such as meditation have been found not only to enhance spiritual centeredness and insight, but also to reduce blood pressure and the negative effects of stress.[4]

In these times of global spiritual transformation, Christians from diverse denominations are reclaiming healing practices as essential to their spiritual formation. Along with their medical and complementary health counterparts, pastors, parish nurses, spiritual healers, and congregational health ministers are exploring the frontiers that lie beyond the wall of separation that has divided spirituality and medicine, and the church and the hospital. With the eclipse of the modern worldview – whose metaphysical vision relegated God to the sidelines, separated mind and body, and limited knowledge to the five senses – a dynamic, relational, and holistic vision of health and healing is emerging.

Within Christian communities, persons are rediscovering God's universal presence, as described in John's gospel. In the spirit of the first chapter of John, they affirm that God's light shines in all things and that wherever healing and truth are present, God's loving light is its source, whether in the laboratory, operating room, sanctuary, or prayer room. The absentee God of the Enlightenment and of Deism has given way to the Galilean image of the compassionate and intimate Healer, whose love embraces and unites every aspect of human life, from diapering babies to caring for the dying. Images of God as a distant, arbitrary potentate, who rewards the faithful and who punishes the infidel, are being replaced by a vision of a God whose nature is defined by the compassion, companionship, and radiant beauty embodied in Jesus the Healer. This vision of God affirms that the Cosmic Healer actively works within the world of the flesh, including the personal flesh of our own bodies, to promote healing and abundant life. The heavens declare the glory and wisdom of God, but so do our lungs, cardiovascular system, brain cells, nervous system, and immune system. Not limited to the narrowly religious realm of life, God is inviting us to become healing companions through medicine, spiritual formation, healing touch, and faithful service.

Within and beyond the church, the healing ministry of Jesus is being rediscovered. No longer viewed as an intellectual embarrassment, 21st-century Christians are "meeting Jesus again for the first time" as they encounter a healer whose compassion, healing touch, and commitment to justice provide a spiritual foundation for the growing interest in complementary medicine and spiritual formation. According to the gospels, Jesus mediated the divine energy of love that transformed people at every level of life and that invited persons to claim their identity as God's beloved children, regardless of their health condition or the social stigmas that had previously defined them as unclean.

Within mainstream and progressive Protestant and Roman Catholic communities of faith, the rediscovery of Jesus the Healer has awakened interest in traditional religious practices, such as laying on of hands and anointing with oil. The healing power of compassionate touch is being claimed in a world in which touch is too often objectifying or even abusive in nature. In addition, many Christians have discovered the healing potential of complementary health practices, such as Janet Mentgen's healing touch and Dolores Krieger's therapeutic touch, to balance, stimulate, and awaken the healing energy in our lives.[5]

Other Christians have discovered the graceful and gentle healing spirit of Mikao Usui's reiki. Joining East and West; and body, mind, and spirit; reiki healing touch enhances personal well-being, reduces pain, and connects us with the universal healing energy that surrounds and permeates us. Reiki is grace in action. Requiring only the intent to be a vehicle of God's healing touch, reiki embodies the dynamic energy of love that animated Jesus' healing ministry.

Yet, despite the growing interest in reiki and other forms of healing touch among Christians, few reiki teachers and practitioners have attempted a creative synthesis of reiki healing touch and traditional Christian understandings of healing and wholeness. In North America, this has led to the false identification of reiki with New Age spirituality among many progressive as well as conservative Christians. While reiki energy is non-sectarian and universal in nature, reiki's gentle touch uniquely manifests the healing ministry of Jesus for our time.

The growing practice of reiki, among Christians and non-Christians alike, is opening up new possibilities for the healing partnership of medical professionals and persons of faith. While reiki is not exclusively Christian and is reputed to have its origins in ancient Buddhist healing practices, reiki's emphasis on our essential vocation as mediators of the divine energy of love and healing reflects the deepest insights of the Christian vision of God as a compassionate, personal, and loving energy field "in whom we live, move, and have our being" (Acts 17:28).

The practice of reiki healing touch challenges Christians to reclaim the healthy spiritual embodiment and energetic healing touch that were central to Jesus' ministry. In its simplicity and universality, reiki healing touch inspires a "priesthood of all healers." While persons' spiritual gifts may vary, reiki affirms that healing power resides in everyone and is not the exclusive possession of a select few, be they Western physicians, traditional shamans, or complementary health care professionals.

Today the church is called to take its rightful place as a leader in the global path that joins spirituality and healing. Among the many paths toward healing and wholeness available to Christians today, reiki gently and creatively incarnates the healing touch of Jesus even as it invites us to explore physical and spiritual healing in its many forms. We believe that the integration of reiki with other traditional Christian practices, such as anointing with oil, liturgical laying on of hands, and intercessory prayer, arises from the same spirit that inspired the Christian universalism reflected in John's gospel. Early Christian seekers of light, and their followers throughout the centuries, were so inspired by the cosmic vision of John's gospel that they embraced truth and healing wherever those things were found, and regardless of the language or techniques used. They found God's light in the Greek language and philosophy that shaped the Gospel of John and the New Testament, as well as in God's continuing covenant with the Hebrew people. Over the centuries, the spiritual children of these first global Christians embraced the full spectrum of God's light and truth as they adopted and transformed non-Christian holy days and practices, such as celebrating the birth of Christ on the same date as the "pagan" celebration of the sun's triumph over darkness, and decorating evergreen trees to honor Christ's birth and eternal blessing of humankind. Touched by God's healing light, they saw God's healing and enlightening presence in both the sacred and secular realms of life. God's healing purposes can be found in pharmaceuticals, psychotherapy, fiction, and song, as well as in the holy scriptures and experiences of worship.

God's healing light shines everywhere and illumines all things. The healing touch of Jesus still nurtures our bodies

and spirits in a variety of ways. Most especially, God's energy of love, embodied in reiki touch, not only transforms
persons, but invites communities of faith to become healing
lights in their neighborhoods.

In the following chapters, we will explore the divine
energy of love as it flows through the healing ministry of
Jesus; the healing liturgies of the church; the life of Mikao
Usui, the spiritual founder of reiki; the practice of reiki and
similar forms of healing touch within the church; and a
variety of spiritual practices that enable us to experience
the touch of God in the midst of our ordinary lives. This
energy of love found in the healing touch of reiki unleashes
a unique chemistry of compassion that transforms pastoral
care, ministry to the dying and chronically ill, and hospital
visitation as well as our own daily prayers.

Reiki healing touch deepens our faith and transforms
our minds, bodies, and spirits. Awakened to Christ's healing touch, we can claim the healing power of God's energy
of love flowing through us, and let our light more brightly
shine in order to bring healing to others, ourselves, and the
planet.

1

THE HEALING LIGHT

*In the beginning was the Word, and the Word
was with God, and the Word was God.... The
Word was in the beginning with God. All things
came into being through the Word, and without
the Word nothing came into being. What has
come into being with the Word was life, and the
life was the light of all people. The light shines in
the darkness and the darkness has not overcome
it... The true light which enlightens everyone
was coming into the Word.*

John 1:1–5, 9

*Then God said, "Let there be light"; and there was
light.*

Genesis 1:3

As children, we learn that the most compelling stories begin with the preface, "Once upon a time."
There is a virtue in the storyteller's chronological
vagueness, for her preface "once upon a time" reminds the
child as well as the adult telling the story that what they are
about to hear is timeless in its truth. In the ecology of life

that seamlessly weaves together past, present, and future, a story's meaning is as real today as it was when it was first told. This is the truth that shines through our cosmic as well as personal narratives.

Once upon a time, the primordial darkness gave birth to light. From the womb of divine creativity, order, and reason, a light burst forth radiating across the universe. Fiery and fecund, lively and expansive, that light was the heart and wisdom of all things. Emerging from the divine matrix, this light gave birth to life in all its variety, beauty, order, and form. As the inner essence of all things, boundless in energy and creativity, this divine power embodied itself in the adventure of galaxies, solar systems, planets, and creatures great and small. Even the darkness was pregnant with light, for, deep down, darkness and light were siblings and partners in the birthing of creation. Yes, once upon a time, and still in every millisecond, the light in which we "live, move, and have our being" brings forth life in all its wonder and abundance. This light was and is the energy of love that constantly births and sustains the universe.

We are the spiritual children of that everlasting light. The light of the first day is our essence and our destiny. The Holy One says, "Let there be light," and a child is born, herself a light of lights, an incarnation of the energy of love, animated in every cell by this continuously creative light. Light from light, love from love, the womb of creation parents forth the universe each moment of the day.

This is the story of cosmic creativity, but it is also the story of the adventure of the spirit among the followers of the light in all times and places. In the spirit of John's gospel, Christians believe that this eternal life and light, the energetic life of creation, found its unique home in Jesus of Nazareth:

"And the Word became flesh and lived among us, and we have seen his glory, the glory of God's only son" (John 1:14).

True to the gospel story, the light also enlightens all persons in every time and place. This very same divine energy of love, incarnate in Jesus Christ, is the love that gives life and wisdom to all things without exception, for nothing can exist without this incarnate light. Throughout the ages, this light has brought forth wise women and wise men, sages and shamans, teachers and physicians, gurus and bodhisattvas, on every continent and among all peoples. Joining East and West, this energetic light is the source of healing and truth in all things. But, once upon a time, and forevermore, this healing light burst forth in the life and influence of Jesus the Healer. The light that shone in Jesus of Nazareth fully illumines Christian history and brings life and healing to all it touches, even beyond the boundaries of Christianity.

It is a sad fact that, true to the narrative from the first chapter of the Gospel of John, persons often prefer darkness to light. Wholeness is forgotten, dualisms emerge, and the original goodness of God's creation is distorted. The message of the Healer, and the energy of love embodied in his healing touch, was even pushed to the periphery of the faith that bears his name. Faith traditions turned their backs on the holiness of embodiment and ordinary life, in the quest for a heavenly realm beyond the flesh.

Forgetting the goodness of creation and the unity of life affirmed by the Healer, church leaders and scientists divorced mind and body from one another. Once spiritual siblings, spirituality and medicine became rivals in the quest for truth and wholeness. The ancient vision of the shaman, whose spiritual leadership embraced religion, medicine, and law, was discarded along with so many of the healing rites and rituals of "primitive" peoples, including our own Hebraic parents. The enchanted world of the lilies of the field and the birds of the air gave way to the vision of the universe as a chaotic and purposeless dance of atomic particles. Stories of the healing touch of the Galilean teacher were discarded as myths, viewed as incomprehensible to anyone who has turned on an electric light or looked through a microscope.

Still, the light of healing shone in the darkness and the darkness could not overcome it. Even as humankind turned away from the energy of love, that universal energy continued to pulse through every cell, bringing healing, insight, and transformation of mind, body, and spirit. Today this lively, healing energy is ours to claim through the practice of reiki healing touch. In the emergence of complementary medicine and global spirituality, the light has once more burst through the closed systems of human thinking, whether they be intellectual, scientific, ethnic, or religious.

THE EMERGENCE OF REIKI

Reiki was initially rediscovered by a mysterious Japanese healer named Mikao Usui. While the story we are about to tell has been recently challenged as factually inaccurate by a number of reiki students, and initially may have been circulated to overcome the bias against the Japanese culture following World War II, it still contains an eternal truth that transcends a purely factual record of the events in question.[1] The story of reiki involves the quest for healing that unites East and West, medicine and spirituality, mysticism and rationalism, action and reflection, personal growth and global healing. Even if the story is not historically accurate, it casts light upon own personal story as we seek to join East and West in order to heal ourselves and our world.

"Once upon a time" at the turn of the 20th century, a young man rose in the ranks of academic and religious life. Educated by Christian missionaries, this young man, Mikao Usui, became headmaster and chaplain in a Christian boys' school in Kyoto, Japan.[2] Following one of the school's chapel services, a group of young men boldly confronted Usui with the following question: "Do you believe that the Bible is God's word?" When Usui answered in the affirmative, they asked him if he could then perform a healing like those attributed to Jesus of Nazareth and his followers. When Usui admitted that he had no healing powers, they challenged his faith and his qualifications to be their spiritual guide.

In response to their query, Usui took the first steps on a spiritual quest for the healing light of Christ. According to this legend, his journey took him to the University of Chicago, where he studied theology and the Bible, and then back to Japan, where he sought the guidance of Buddhist teachers. Though Usui sought the wisdom of both East and West, neither the spiritual teachings of Buddhism nor the rationalism of liberal Protestant Christianity satisfied his quest to embody the healing ministry of Jesus in his own life and ministry.

The liberal Protestantism of the early 20th century held that the miracles of Jesus violated the laws of nature and were no longer relevant to modern persons in light of the findings of science and biblical scholarship. At that time, conservative and liberal Christians agreed on one thing: if you're sick, you see a doctor; there is no need to rely on divine intervention to bring healing to your life. While conservative Christians believed in the scriptural witness to Jesus' miracles, they also claimed that the primary purpose

of Jesus' healing ministry was to establish Jesus' identity as
the Son of God. Now that the church is fully established and
mediates the good news of salvation, it no longer needs the
bulwark of divine healing to affirm that Jesus is the Savior,
they declared. Conservative Christians saw concern for
physical healing as distracting persons from the true focus
of faith – the call to conversion and our heavenly destination
as God's redeemed children.

Usui was also frustrated by the attitudes of Buddhist
monks, who admitted that while Gautama the Buddha may
have healed persons, physical healing must now be left to
physicians. The quest for enlightenment, they believed,
took humans beyond the concern for the body and its well-
being.

Despite these setbacks, Usui continued to seek the keys to
healing energy. He continued to search for ancient Buddhist
healing texts. He believed that somewhere hidden in the ancient texts of Christianity and Buddhism he would find the
secret to a healing path for the modern world. Usui eventually discovered a number of ancient healing symbols from
Tibetan Buddhism, but he initially found no way to employ
them. Undeterred, Usui sought an answer to his prayers by
fasting and meditation.

In the solitude of a mountain near Kyoto, Japan, Usui
silently opened himself to divine guidance. On the 21st day
of his retreat, according to one reiki story, a light burst forth
from the heavens. Hurtling across the horizon, this light
struck Usui on the forehead, causing him to lose consciousness. When he regained consciousness, Usui remembered
that the light enveloped and transmitted the meaning of the
ancient healing symbols that he had been studying. At that
moment, he understood that the way to share the energy of

love was through the spiritual practice of laying on of hands. A path that was eventually to join East and West in the quest for healing was rediscovered. Though grounded in Japanese culture and Buddhist healing practice, reiki complemented and provided a way to mediate the healing touch of Jesus of Nazareth.

HEALING FIRE IN THE WEST

The quest for the energy of love is never a solitary one. True to another visionary concept – "the hundredth monkey" – when a great truth is discovered in one place, it springs forth almost immediately somewhere else. Indeed, as Usui began his quest for divine healing, small groups of Christians also sought a deeper experience of God's healing Spirit. In the first few decades of the 20th century, this energy burst forth as a fire from heaven among what eventually became known as the Pentecostal movement in America.[3] Like Usui, these American Pentecostals sought to transcend the rationalistic orientation of contemporary religion in order to embrace a fully embodied spirituality in which every aspect of human life became a focus for divine healing. At Azuza Street Church in Los Angeles, California, and then across the globe, Pentecostals embraced God's healing fire through non-rational experiences, such as speaking in tongues, mystic visions and prophecies, and healing touch.

In the Pentecostal movement, God's healing light encompassed all persons, regardless of ethnicity or gender. Barriers of mind, body, and spirit were overcome. Awakened to the universal energy of love, the words of the prophets and early Christians came alive and often challenged the conservative theology of those who experienced God's healing fire:

I will pour my Spirit upon all flesh,
and your sons and daughters shall prophesy,
and your young men shall see visions,
and your old men shall dream dreams.

Acts 2:17

Yet God's healing fire was not limited to the lively and ecstatic practices of Pentecostal Christianity. A few decades later in the 20th century, a small band of seekers within mainline Protestant churches, including Episcopalian Agnes Sanford and Methodists Olga and Ambrose Worrall, rediscovered a healing path that would come to embrace the insights of science, medicine, and faith. While affirming the best of Western science and biblical scholarship, they believed that God is the source of the wonders of medicine as well as the power of faith to transform people's lives. They affirmed that the light of God, spoken of in terms of the Divine Word and Wisdom, was the gentle wellspring of truth and healing wherever they are found. They believed that after years of dormancy, God's Spirit was ready to burst forth in new and surprising ways within the more structured worship of mainstream Christianity. Like Mikao Usui, they believed that God's healing light was still shining, despite the forgetfulness of mainstream Christianity. They claimed that Jesus' promise to his first-century disciples applied to men and women in our time, and that God's aim was toward wholeness and creativity at every level of life.[4]

These spiritual adventurers believed that divine healing complemented medical healing, and that by opening to God persons would experience the healing promises of Jesus animating their own lives in new and surprising ways.

Believe me that I am in the [Parent] and the
[Parent] is in me; but if you do not, then believe
me because of the works themselves. Very truly,
I tell you, the one who believes in me will also do
the works that I do and, in fact, will do greater
works than these, because I am going to the
[Parent].

John 14:11–12

"You can do greater works!" Christ's promise astounded those who sought to revive the healing movement in mainstream churches and it astounds us still today. The healing power of the universe, the divine creativity that enlivens every cell, is at our fingertips to bless and to heal individuals and institutions. Non-dramatic acts of worship, touch, imagination, and compassion open the door to an inflow of divine energy, to heal the sick and to bring guidance to the lost.

CONNECTING WITH THE VINE

Jesus once told a story of vines and branches. These words describe the dynamics of our relationship with the divine energy of God and the goal of our healing journey today.

I am the true vine, and my [Parent] is the
vinegrower. God removes every branch in me
that bears no fruit. Every branch that bears
fruit, God prunes to make it bear more fruit. You
have already been cleansed by the word that I
have spoken to you. Abide in me as I abide in
you. Just as the branch cannot bear fruit by
itself unless it abides in the vine, neither can you
unless you abide in me. I am the vine, you are

the branches. Those who abide in me and I in them bear much fruit, because apart from me you can do nothing. Whoever does not abide in me is thrown away like a branch and withers; such branches are gathered, thrown into the fire, and burned. If you abide in me, and my words abide in you, ask for whatever you wish, and it will be done for you. My [Parent] is glorified by this, that you bear much fruit and become my disciples. As the [Parent] has loved me, so I have loved you, abide in my love.

John 15:1–9

Jesus' words describe what happens when we are connected with the divine energy of love, which, like the sap flowing through a vine, gives life and fruitfulness to all things. Without that spiritual energy, we perish. If we turn from God's healing energy, we wither from lack of spiritual and relational nourishment. But the wisdom of John's gospel also tells us that even in our turning from the divine, God's light follows us – God's light flows through our lives inviting us to claim the divine path to health and wholeness available to us today in the growing partnership of medicine and spirituality. When we open ourselves to the energy of love in all its diverse forms, our lives will bear fruit in great abundance.

Reiki healing touch is one way we can open to the energetic flow of God's love. When we practice reiki healing touch, the life-giving energy of the vine flows through us to those we touch.

Combined with prayer, meditation, worship, scriptural reflection, rituals of healing, and commitment to service, reiki enables us to awaken to God's universal energy flowing through our lives and the world. Reiki is a form of body prayer, joining healing touch, generosity of spirit, and openness to God's movement in our lives. Reiki embodies and focuses God's energy of love, which flows through every branch of the vine. Bathed in that loving energy, we experience peace, wholeness, balance, and inspiration. We experience the divine generosity that permeates all of creation – Christian and Buddhist, human and non-human – with its loving and transforming energy.

THE MIRACLES OF HEALING

In the language of the New Testament, the word "miracle" points to divine "acts of power" and "signs and wonders." In contrast to the modern understanding of a miracle as a supernatural violation of the laws of nature, the biblical tradition understands the world in its entirety as a reflection of divine activity. The world is an open system in which God is not an external intruder, but an intimate presence. With Walt Whitman, the biblical sages understood that "all is miracle."

Though God is present everywhere, some moments nevertheless reveal God's care in unique and powerful ways. In light of the interplay of divine universality and personality, Christians can affirm that God was uniquely, though not solely, present in Jesus of Nazareth, the Healing Christ. Jesus' death and resurrection reveal God's compassion and desire that all creation experience abundant life.

Today we can experience these same signs and wonders through reiki healing touch. Like intercessory prayer, meditation and visualization, laying on of hands, Holy Communion, and loving service, reiki truly transforms bodies, spirits, and relationships. Generally gentle and undramatic in nature, the practice of reiki promotes well-being at every level of life.

According to the story of the origins of reiki, as he walked down the mountain following his life-transforming experience, Usui stubbed his toe on a rock. Inspired by his recent vision, Usui touched his wounded toe and experienced an immediate sense of well-being and a cessation of pain. To him, this was a miracle! Later in the day, Usui met a young girl suffering from a toothache. Usui asked permission to touch her cheek. As he touched her, her swelling diminished and her pain ceased. To that young girl, reiki's gentle touch was a miracle!

These gentle miracles of healing and wholeness happen every day in the practice of reiki. Recently, Kate's mother, Maxine, asked Bruce to give her a reiki treatment for a persistent toothache. Since it was Friday afternoon and dental offices were closed for the weekend, she was worried about spending the next few days in excruciating pain. She felt that reiki might be the only way to ease her discomfort. At her request, Bruce laid hands on her for ten minutes, simply letting divine healing energy flow to the source of her pain. She felt an immediate sense of comfort and well-being. The pain disappeared for nearly a week, giving her a respite until she was able to obtain the services of her dentist. While reiki did not eliminate the need for dental treatment, reiki touch brought her the relief she needed in order to go about her daily tasks.

It is clear that the gentle energy of reiki healing touch supports medical healing. Following heart bypass surgery, an orthopedic surgeon sought reiki treatment from one of his medical colleagues. In the course of several reiki treatments, he experienced a relief from pain and an enhancement of vital energy. Years later, when he was diagnosed with yet another life-threatening illness, he sought the treatment of other reiki practitioners, including us. Today, he attributes his remission from cancer to an interplay of medical care, personal optimism, a supportive spouse, the prayers of others, and the reiki treatments he received. He believes that reiki, along with the prayers of friends, focused and intensified the impact of the standard Western medical treatments he received, and that together these factors saved his life. It is appropriate that his own medical practice now embodies high-touch as well as high-tech approaches to healing.

Kate taught one of Bruce's reiki students how to administer self-reiki following the shattering of her shin bone. Her initial request was simply for pain relief. She applied reiki daily over her cast. Not only did she experience a reduction in pain, but, according to her physician, her bones knit together in half the expected time.

During her chemotherapy treatments, another of Bruce's reiki students, Susan, gave herself reiki healing touch as she envisaged God's healing light permeating her body. Between chemotherapy treatments, she received reiki treatments from Kate and continued with her own self-reiki. Susan experienced few of the typical unpleasant side effects from her chemotherapy. Instead, she felt energized throughout the whole process. Today Susan maintains that "I couldn't have made it without prayer, visualization, and reiki. Reiki was the perfect complement to the chemotherapy. The healing light of reiki, along with the prayers of my church, gave me hope in difficult times, as well as a sense of personal agency throughout the medical process."

No one can control, predict, or fully understand the healing process. But children as well as adults find wholeness through the healing touch of reiki. A 13-year-old whom Kate treated for a painful foot injury greeted her mother following a treatment with the acclamation, "Kate is a good minister! She touched my foot and took away the pain."

The biblical tradition speaks of Daniel discovering the protective presence of God in the lion's den. The reiki healing touch that gently addresses bodily ailments can also be the source of confidence and courage in the midst of personal challenges. The healing touch of reiki reminds us that we are surrounded by God's care wherever we are, and that we have the resources to face whatever lies ahead for us.

In her early 40s, Wendy was overwhelmed by the turmoil and conflict that characterized her workplace. For a while, she felt like quitting and began each day with a sense of foreboding that eventually manifested itself in physical symptoms and absenteeism. Although she was active in her United Church of Christ congregation, she lacked any practical tools for bringing the insights of her faith to the problems of daily life. In her own words, "My faith was just head faith. I believed in God, the Holy Trinity, and the Creeds of the Church, but they didn't make any difference in my work life or relationships. When I learned reiki, everything changed. I saw the connection between body, mind, and spirit, and knew that I no longer needed to be the victim of office politics." Each day, as she prepared for work, Wendy gave herself a ten-minute reiki treatment and envisaged herself surrounded by God's protective and healing light. Whenever she began to feel anxiety at the workplace, Wendy simply touched herself with the spirit of God's presence in reiki.

Over the next few months, Wendy found the courage and the strength not only to continue working, but also to become an agent of change and justice in her workplace.

"God touched me and made me whole," Wendy affirms. "I knew that the reiki energy came from God and that God was with me each step of the way, circling and sustaining me with protective love."

As he lay dying of AIDS, Tom felt alone and touch-deprived. His spirit withered as his body wasted away. At first, he was dubious when his friend George, a lay leader at a local Methodist church, offered to arrange for him to receive reiki treatments from a practitioner in their church. He was surprised that a Christian would be practicing reiki. He thought reiki was just another New Age gimmick. He wondered what reiki had to do with Christianity and whether the Christianity of his childhood faith experience – one that judged his sexual orientation and saw AIDS as divine punishment for sinful behavior – could be of any help to him now that he was dying. But Tom was willing to try anything just to ease his pain of body and spirit. As George and members of the healing team gave him reiki treatments over the next several months, Tom experienced a profound physical and spiritual transformation. He felt physically connected to others once more. Yet he also experienced a spiritual peace that permeated his whole being. In the words of theologian and Bible scholar Marcus Borg, Tom met "Jesus again for the first time" through the gentle touch and constancy of his new friends. The "body of Christ" (1 Corinthians 12) became real to Tom through reiki healing touch and a community of caring Christians whose love welcomed him into the circle of healing. In his dying, Tom found new life and wholeness and companionship with the God whose love embraces mind, body, spirit, and relationships.

The healing light of Christ shines in every life and through every compassionate touch. God's energy of love flows through the hands of reiki practitioners and revives persons spiritually and physically in amazing ways. Reiki is a gift of God to the world, and a blessing to a church in search of a healing path that embraces Western and complementary medicine, spiritual formation, and the lively pluralism of our time.

2

THE HEALING CHRIST

Now there was a woman who had been suffering from hemorrhages for twelve years. She had endured much under many physicians, and had spent all that she had; and she was no better, but rather grew worse. She had heard about Jesus and came up behind him in the crowd and touched his cloak, for she said, "If I but touch his clothes, I will be made well." Immediately, her hemorrhage stopped; and she felt in her body that she was healed of her disease. Immediately aware that power had gone forth from him, Jesus turned about in the crowd and said, "Who touched my clothes?" And his disciples said to him, "You see the crowd pressing in on you; how can you say, 'Who touched me?'" He looked all around to see who had done it. But the woman, knowing what had happened to her, came in fear and trembling, fell down before him, and told him the whole truth. He said to her, "Daughter, your faith has made you well; go in peace, and be healed of your disease."

Mark 5:25–34

Jesus the Healer is being rediscovered throughout the Christian community. For some persons, Jesus comes alive as the winds of the Spirit burst forth in strange tongues and mystic visions. But for many more, the door to God's healing presence is being opened by an exciting, new vision of reality, which embraces quantum particles, energy events, holograms, and non-local causation. For others, an encounter with the universal energy described and practiced by traditional Chinese medicine allows them to see Jesus for the first time as a unique mediator and transformer of the energy (*chi*) of the universe. Still others, with chronic pain or life-threatening illness, cry out in need, like the woman with the hemorrhage, and experience Christ's presence as the answer to their prayers. By whatever means, persons are still being healed and transformed by God's energy of love. The light of Christ shines anew in their lives and invites them to experience themselves and God in surprising and powerful ways.

Healing was the heart and soul of Jesus' ministry. Long before the emergence of whole-person medicine in the West, Jesus, the Jewish healer, saw human beings in terms of their original wholeness. For Jesus, body, mind, and spirit interpenetrate one another seamlessly. Social relationships shape not only our faith, but also our health. Jesus knew that a change in one area of our lives can transform every other aspect of our lives. Jesus believed that God's intimate love for the world is reflected in the divine desire to respond to suffering in all of its manifestations.

Jesus' first public pronouncements set the agenda for a ministry that came to embrace the totality of his life. Quoting the prophet Isaiah (61:1–2), Jesus announced his mission to the hometown congregation at Nazareth.

The Spirit of the Lord is upon me, because he has anointed me to bring good news to the poor. He has sent me to proclaim release to the captives, and recovery of the sight to the blind, to let the oppressed go free, to proclaim the year of the Lord's favor.

Luke 4:18–19

When the disciples of the imprisoned John the Baptist asked if Jesus was the one whose coming their teacher had announced, Jesus responded,

Go and tell John what you hear and see: the blind receive their sight, the lame walk, the lepers are cleansed, the deaf hear, and the poor have good news brought to them.

Matthew 11:4–5

While virtually all the founders of the world's great religions were endowed with extraordinary spiritual powers, Jesus alone placed whole-person healing at the forefront of his message, with his affirmation that God's abundant life embraced the totality of a person's existence.

The healing of the whole person in this lifetime was essential to Jesus' message. While we are destined for eternal communion with God in a realm that has neither beginning nor end, we are also invited to experience the fullness of life right here and now. Innovative biblical scholar Marcus Borg confirms the centrality of Jesus' healing ministry: "Behind this picture of Jesus as a healer and exorcist...I see the claim that Jesus performed paranormal healings and exorcisms as history remembered. Indeed more healings are told about

Jesus than any other figure in the Jewish tradition. He must have been a remarkable healer."[1] According to Morton Kelsey, who pioneered healing ministries in the Episcopalian church, "forty-one instances of physical and mental healing are recorded in the four gospels" and "nearly one-fifth of the entire gospels is devoted to Jesus' healing and discussions occasioned by it."[2] When Jesus encountered people, "a power went forth from him" that transformed their minds, bodies, spirits, relationships, and social standing.

THE HEBRAIC ROOTS OF
JESUS' HEALING MINISTRY

Jesus' healing ministry was grounded in a creative dialogue with the religious tradition of his parents. Despite his controversies with certain Jewish religious leaders, Jesus constantly affirmed his Jewish roots and saw them as definitive of his own healing ministry, even when he proposed alternative understandings of divine activity and ritual behavior. When Jesus called his faith tradition to transformation, he did so as a loyal son who desired that his faith tradition truly reflect God's vision for humankind.

In order to claim authentically the energy of love that was at the heart of Jesus' ministry, we must first explore the Hebraic worldview that was foundational for Jesus' own vision of reality. Jesus' healing ministry was the embodiment of the Hebraic hope for shalom and wholeness. At the heart of Hebraic worldview lie the following affirmations.

1. *God is the wise and loving creator of heaven and earth.* All things have their origin in the loving care of God. The heavens declare the glory of God and so do our bodies. Humankind is "fearfully and wonderfully made" (Psalm 139:14). God's handiwork is seen in the lilies of the field

and in the birds of the air. God's energy of love creates the planets, human life, and the non-human world. Every aspect of the universe reflects the love and intelligence of its Creator.

2. *Creation is "very good" in its entirety.* As reflections of divine wisdom, we can rejoice in physical exercise, sexuality, healthy food, good work, parenting, friendship, love, and creativity. The body is a reflection of God's love and intelligence and is essential to our spiritual growth. Accordingly, spiritual formation involves claiming the holiness of the body and affirming God's presence in everyday events. God can be experienced in marriage, parenting, work, and play.

3. *Human existence is holistic in nature.* Human existence is a multidimensional and intricate interplay of body, mind, spirit, and relationships. Each aspect of life shapes and conditions and is, conversely, shaped by all the others. Spiritual well-being includes not only a commitment to prayer and meditation, but also to healthy eating habits, exercise, and rest. Health involves loving interpersonal relationships, as well a commitment to achieving justice in the social order, and beauty in the environment. As the prophets proclaim, social justice is essential both to our physical well-being and to our ability to hear the word of God. Those who turn away from their neighbor's needs may ultimately experience a "famine of hearing the word of God" (Amos 8:11–12). Salvation, or wholeness, is communal as well as individual. Eternity pertains to the body as well as to the spirit.

4. *Human existence is "very good," but not "perfect." Accordingly, a good life includes sickness and death as well as health and vitality.* Sickness is a reality with which all persons must

eventually contend. The traditional Hebraic explanations for sickness and disease maintained that sickness was ultimately related to alienation from God, unjust social relations, and immoral behavior. According to one stream of Hebraic thought, the righteous prosper, while the sinful are punished with sickness and poverty. Yet another stream, reflected in the Book of Job, challenges the linear one-to-one correspondence of behaviors and outcomes. Even the righteous suffer, Job asserts, while the sinful often rest comfortably in their beds and fine houses.

As he reflected on his own tradition's understandings of sickness and poverty, Jesus took the view of the author of Job and directly challenged the viewpoint that individual sin is the sole source of a person's physical or mental illness (John 9:1–7).

5. *Certain diseases rendered persons "unclean" and, accordingly, barred them from ordinary activities, such as participation in public worship and living among their families and peers.* The woman with the flow of blood could not, for example, attend worship, sit on furniture that others would use, go to the city well at the appointed hours, or engage in an intimate relationship with her husband. Lepers, tax collectors, foreigners, and prostitutes were outcasts whose presence in public worship contaminated the synagogue or temple and might lead to God's departure from those holy shrines. According to this viewpoint, sickness was not so much a matter of contagion, but of purity and holiness. Judged as unclean, many persons suffered not only from the physical pain of disease, but also from the theologically rooted social stigma that left them spiritually, socially, and economically uprooted and homeless.

6. *Because of the association of medicine with pagan religions, the Hebraic tradition was ambivalent about seeking the assistance of physicians and other medical professionals.* According to the Hebraic tradition, God was the ultimate healer and source of life and death. Given the moral dimensions of illness, it was more essential to prepare spiritually than to respond medically to illness. The fruits of repentance, a clear conscience, and righteous behavior restore persons to well-being. Further, contact with foreign physicians might compromise the faithful, who might regain their health, but lose their relationship with God. Despite this ambivalence about physicians and pharmaceuticals, positive contacts with Greco-Roman physicians and a growing sense of God's universal revelation led to the recognition that God is the source of medical knowledge and care.

> *Honor physicians for their services, for the Eternal created them; for their gift comes from the Most High... God created medicines out of the earth, and the sensible will not despise them. Was not water made sweet with a tree in order that its power might be known? And God gave skill to human beings that God might be glorified in the divine's marvelous works. By them the physician heals and takes away pain; the pharmacist makes a mixture from them.*
> Sirach 38:1–2, 4–8a

7. *Despite their ambivalence about God's role in healing and sickness, the Hebraic people believed that God acted in the lives of individuals to bring health and wholeness to every level of existence.* God acted in history, delivering the Hebrews

from captivity and guiding them to the promised land. As the stories of the patriarchs, matriarchs, and early Hebraic judges reveal, God also worked in persons' lives to restore fertility, cleanse leprosy, and awaken the dead. While personal healings were rarely recorded in the Hebraic scriptures, most Jewish religious leaders believed that God was at work in our personal and corporate lives and could deliver persons and nations from disease and captivity.

In conclusion, while Jesus' parents in the faith were often ambivalent about the role of God in health and sickness, they affirmed without question that God was active in the world, and that our attitudes and behaviors in relationship to God and God's commandments could bring either health or illness. As a child of this rich religious heritage, Jesus framed his innovative and compassionate message of healing and salvation in light of the prevalent attitudes of his religious companions.

JESUS' HEALING MINISTRY

Jesus came down with them and stood on a level place, with a great crowd of his disciples and a great multitude of people from all Judea, Jerusalem, and the coast of Tyre and Sidon. They had come to hear him and to be healed of their diseases; and those who were troubled with unclean spirits were cured. And all in the crowd were trying to touch him, for power came out from him and healed all of them.

Luke 6:17–19

Jesus was a pulsing center of divine power and energy. Like an electrical transformer, the energy of love flowed from Jesus toward persons in need of physical, relational, emotional, and spiritual healing. The power that emanated from his touch and presence was akin to the power of the big birth and the first light of creation, the primal energy that penetrates the darkness and brings forth life from God's womb of creativity. Grounded in his unity with God, Jesus was the connective "vine" through whom God's life-giving energy flowed abundantly to everyone he touched.

Jesus' healing was profoundly personal and intimate in nature. It embraced the whole of a person's life and not merely her or his physical symptoms. Even those who were troubled by painful physical ailments knew that a physical cure or alleviation of symptoms was not enough to bring them wholeness. Many came to Jesus in search of transformation of their minds as well as their bodies.

In addition, it is helpful to know that Jesus used a variety of healing methods – touch, the spoken word, prayer and distant healing, spittle and mud, exorcism, and personal challenge. Recognizing the uniqueness of each person and the multidimensional nature of health and illness, Jesus used whatever means would be most helpful to the one who stood before him. He did not compel persons to become well, but invited them to claim the healing that was God's will for their lives as reflected in their deepest spiritual desires. Jesus asked questions of persons in need of wholeness, such as "What do you want me to do for you?" or "Do you want to be healed?" Jesus recognized that wholeness cannot be coerced, but must be accepted and embraced, consciously or unconsciously, at the right time and place.

We are fortunate that Jesus did *not* practice, teach, or recommend only *one* method of healing. Jesus' many-faceted style of healing gives us the freedom to seek healing and wholeness by whatever means are appropriate, convenient, and requested by the person in need. As we stated before, wherever there is healing and truth, God is its ultimate source. God, whose creativity and love is manifest in every cell of our bodies and in every loving thought, can use any method to bring wholeness to ourselves or another. Accordingly, followers of Jesus' way of healing can employ surgery, medication, and chemotherapy, but they can also utilize acupuncture, chiropractic, massage, therapeutic touch, and reiki.

Still we can gain much by reflecting on the gospel accounts of Jesus' healing, even though we recognize that the gospels only give a glimpse of the fullness of Jesus' ministry of wholeness and love. As John's gospel notes, "But there are also many other things that Jesus did; if every one of them were written down, I suppose the world itself could not contain all the books that would be written" (John 21: 25). In meditating on Jesus' healing ministry, we find the inspiration to become vehicles of divine healing in the 21st century. In the following paragraphs, we will reflect on the many dimensions of Jesus' healing ministry.

The healing power of love

The New Testament proclaims that Jesus is the incarnation of divine love for humankind and the planet. Jesus' healings were inspired by the love that seeks abundance for all things. Dietrich Bonhoeffer once stated that "only a suffering God can save." Jesus felt from the inside the physical and relational pain of persons with paralysis, mental illness, and leprosy. He experienced the spiritual alienation of tax collectors, whose wealth could not drive away feelings of inferiority and meaninglessness. He embraced as sisters and

friends women who were forced by economic and social conditions to choose prostitution as a means of employment, or
who were rendered voiceless in a patriarchal society. Jesus'
compassion called him to nurture people's bodies and spirits
alike – to feed 5,000 hungry followers and to give the spiritually malnourished the bread of life.

Jesus often healed persons by addressing the underlying
social conditions that create illness of body and spirit. In a
world defined by standards of purity and impurity, Jesus
welcomed everyone into his circle of love and wholeness.
Jesus welcomed lonely and lost "outcasts" with the same
care with which he embraced powerful and wealthy persons,
whose despair and feelings of meaninglessness overcame
their own antagonism toward this unorthodox healer.

Jesus healed by *loving* people into health and by *listening*
them into life. The barriers constructed by society and by their
own minds could not separate them from his care. He saw
life and health where others saw death and brokenness. In
speaking of Jesus' hospitality to the sick and disenfranchised,
New Testament scholar John Dominic Crossan states that
"the Kingdom of God as a process of open commensality,
of a nondiscriminating table depicting in miniature a
nondiscriminating society, clashes fundamentally with honor
and shame, those basic values of the ancient Mediterranean
culture and society."[3] While I disagree with Crossan's assertion
that "Jesus could not or did not cure that disease [leprosy]
or any other one," he correctly notes the power of love to
transform the lives of persons alienated from society by their
physical ailments. According to Crossan, Jesus healed the
leper's illness (see Mark 1:40–44) and other socially taboo
illnesses "by refusing to accept the disease's ritual uncleanness
or social ostracization." The true miracle in this and other

healings, Crossan contends, involves the transformation of the social world, involves breaking down the barriers between clean and unclean, and welcome and unwelcome.[4]

However we explain the many dimensions of Jesus' healing ministry, there is no doubt that love, acceptance, and affirmation can transform our self-understanding and place in society. But in the intricate interplay of mind, body, and spirit, love can also transform "the molecules of emotion" that course through our bodies, and can restore us to physical well-being.[5]

Transforming touch

When the woman with the hemorrhage touched Jesus, a power went forth from him. In countless ways, touch can change our lives. Without touch, we – like newborn babies – wither and die physically and spiritually. As the largest organ of the body, the skin is nurtured by healthy connectedness with others. Massage, hugs, caresses, sexual intimacy, holding, and reiki all convey to us the energy of love that nurtures our whole being. Touch can heal, but tragically many children and adults experience unwelcome, manipulative, alienating, objectifying, and toxic touch. Others are starved for touch and healthy physical intimacy.

Jesus' ministry models healthy professional touch. Jesus touched others from the wellspring of love and compassion. He did not force his healing touch on others and he touched them only for their well-being and with their permission. But when he touched persons, a healing power went forth from his hands that transformed every aspect of their lives.

Nearly half of the recorded healings in the gospels involve Jesus touching or being touched. Jesus held children, and touched deaf ears, blind eyes, festering skin, and mute tongues. Jesus touched the clean and the unclean, women and men alike.

Although the scriptures do not describe any single methodology of healing touch that was characteristic of Jesus' ministry, we suspect that his touch was personal and situational in nature. Jesus may have lovingly caressed the heads of the children who sat on his lap. With adults, Jesus may have touched the point of physical impairment, such as the eyes or ears of persons experiencing blindness or deafness. He may also have simply touched with open palms their foreheads, shoulders, and back in the spirit of today's ritual of laying on of hands. While there is no biblical evidence, Jesus' touch may even have balanced the energy fields surrounding persons' bodies, in a manner characteristic of today's practices of reiki, and of therapeutic and healing touch.

One thing is certain; Jesus' touch was supportive, welcome, loving, and healing for women and men alike. In a world which, then and now, abuses women through harassing and objectifying touch, Jesus' affirmation of women as disciples and equals clearly reveals that his touch of women empowered them physically, spiritually, and socially.

Jesus also allowed himself to be touched, both physically and spiritually, by women as well as by men. The woman suffering from the hemorrhage simply touched his garment and was made whole. Jesus was not even consciously aware of her touch or her malady. Yet this abundant healing energy of love surged forth to cure her disease and restore her spirit. Jesus' openness to God and to others created a healing environment that did not require his conscious effort or awareness. The same is true for us. Grace flows though us, whether or not we are mindful of it, when we consistently open ourselves to God's healing light. Divine healing arises from our willingness to let others touch us in such a way that we receive their pain as well as their gifts.

The power of the Word

In the biblical tradition, the truth, life, and love of God flows through the divine Word. The universe is created by the vibrant and energetic Word of God. Accordingly, human words were not accidental, but pointed to the spiritual reality of a place or a person. A person's name, for instance, designated something important about their deepest identity. Beneath his vacillating behavior, Peter was truly a "solid rock." Changing your name – from Saul to Paul, or from Jacob to Israel, for example – revealed the reality of a new orientation in life.

In that same spirit, Jesus used words to heal the sick and to invite persons to discover their deepest desires. To the man who lay paralyzed at the pool for 38 years, Jesus asks, "Do you want to be made well?" When the man responds with excuses for his predicament, Jesus issues a life-changing command: "Stand up, take your mat, and walk" (John 5:1–9). Using mud and saliva, Jesus gently massages the eyes of a young man blind from birth and then instructs him and his parents to "go wash in the pool of Siloam" (John 9:1–7). To the question posed by a man with a skin disease, "Lord, if you choose, you can make me clean," Jesus responds, "I do choose. Be made clean" (Luke 5:12–16).

Jesus invited people to reflect on their relationship to God as means of opening the door to healing. To two men who were blind, Jesus asks, "Do you believe that I am able to do this?" In response to their affirmation, Jesus declares, "According to your faith let it be done to you" (Matthew 9: 27–31).

Jesus questioned the demonic realities that possessed the man of the Gerasenes. He asked who they were and what they wanted, and gave this "legion" of demons their heart's desire, in order to liberate the man from the shackles of a fragmented personality. Jesus' words of exorcism delivered persons from the bondage of epilepsy and mental illness.

Through questions, invitations, and commands, Jesus' words transformed people's lives. Our words shape our perception of reality and, consequently, can heal or destroy bodies and souls. In contrast to those who place limits on possibility and who deny hope in the order to promote what they assume to be realism, Jesus' life-affirming words created a healing possibility for persons in need. His words lovingly vibrated through the deepest recesses of people's lives, bringing healing and new life. Jesus' realism included the realities of illness and death, but also the equally powerful realities of God's healing touch and abiding presence.

The importance of action

Jesus also clearly invited persons to become partners in their healing process. Calls to action always accompanied Jesus' healings. To a man, who – because he was paralyzed – was lowered from the rooftop in order receive Jesus' touch, the Healer commands, "Stand up, take your mat and go to your home" (Mark 2:1–12). Jesus invited Matthew the tax collector to a new way of life with the words, "Follow me" (Matthew 9:9).

We are called to be active co-creators with God in mending the world and in bringing healing to ourselves and to others. Like a good parent, Jesus empowered persons to embrace a larger, more dynamic vision of themselves, and then to act on their visions. As one who himself grew in wisdom and in stature, Jesus empowered others to grow and to mature in claiming their own fullest possible stature as healthy and loving children of God.

The power of faith to heal

Today physicians speak of the impact of our beliefs on our overall well-being. They call the power of the mind to shape our health the "placebo effect." Candace Pert suggests that peptides, the molecules of emotion, are found not only in our brains, but throughout our body.[6] Not only does the mind have a body, but the body has a mind. Our thoughts and feelings are instantaneously translated into chemical reactions. Hope, faith, and service enliven the body and enhance the immune system. Fear, hopelessness, stress, and alienation depress the immune system and tax the cardiovascular system.

In his words and actions, Jesus provided images of hope and healing for persons in spiritual, emotional, and physical need. The woman with the hemorrhage heard words that validated her experience of divine power. As she walked toward Jesus, the object of her faith and hope, she said to herself, "If I but touch his clothes, I will be made well." After the power of divine energy filled her being, Jesus pronounced a final word of healing: "Daughter, your faith has made you well; go in peace and be healed of your disease" (Mark 5:25–34).

On another occasion, Jesus saw the faith of the men who brought their paralyzed friend to receive his healing touch. Undeterred by the obstacles that lay in their way, they focused only the healing power of God. Their faith inspired them to create a new path to Jesus – they tore open the roof and lowered their friend down to Jesus. They were pioneers in the movement to make places of worship accessible to persons with disabilities. As the scripture states, "When he saw their faith, he said to the paralytic, 'Take heart, son, your sins are forgiven,'" and then, "Stand up, take your bed, and go to your home" (Mark 2:1–12).

The healing power of forgiveness

While Jesus did not identify a one-to-one correspondence between sin and sickness, he recognized that guilt, sin, and shame could paralyze mind, body, and spirit. To the man lowered from the rooftop to Jesus by his friends, Jesus pronounces the forgiveness that allows him to go on with life as a whole person. To those who crucify him, Jesus proclaims, "Father, forgive them; for they do not know what they are doing" (Luke 23:34).

Forgiveness mediates the unmerited love of God to us and enables us to reclaim our identity as God's beloved children. Freed from the burdens of the past, we can become a new creation and seek reconciliation with those we have harmed.

The power of the imagination to heal

Jesus gently lured people to experience reality from God's perspective. The God of mustard seeds, improbable births, hidden treasures, and silently growing seeds invites persons to imaginatively envision their full potential as beloved, worthy, and empowered children of God. When Jairus' friends persist in maintaining that his 12-year-old daughter is dead, Jesus puts them out of the house and permits only the parents and his closest male disciples to accompany him to the girl's room. Where the crowd saw only death, Jesus saw a girl in a coma, who could be revived to life in all its abundance. Jesus created a healing environment by challenging the preconceived limitations of the mourners.

He believed that faith opens persons to a deeper vision of reality and to a greater manifestation of divine power. Jesus enabled persons to see the divine possibilities in themselves, often hidden by social norms and limiting attitudes, and then to boldly live out of that larger awareness.

Distance makes no difference in healing

Jesus was not limited by space, time, or social divisions. Though the centurion was an instrument of foreign oppression, Jesus responded to his plea on behalf of his servant, as scripture notes.

> *When Jesus heard this [the man's words of faith] he was amazed at him, and turning to the crowd that followed him, he said, "I tell you, not even in Israel have I found such faith." When those who had been sent returned to the house, they found the slave in good health.*
>
> Luke 7:9–10

In healing the Syrophoenician woman's daughter, both Jesus and the woman overcame barriers of time, space, gender, ethnicity, and spiritual alienation. In response to the woman's boldness, Jesus exorcised the demons that tormented her child.

> *Then he said to her, "For saying that, you may go – the demon has left your daughter." So she went home, found the child lying on the bed, and the demon gone.*
>
> Mark 7:24–30

Today physicians and physicists speak of holograms, holomovements, and non-local causation as evidence that the universe is a vast web of relationships, in which parts and the whole are intricately connected. In the ecology of wholeness and healing, our thoughts and prayers radiate across the universe and create a healing environment that promotes the well-being of others. Researchers study the benefits of intercessory prayer and distant healing techniques on cardiac patients, plants, mice, and fungi, and find that, in ways that we cannot explain, prayer changes things for the best.[7]

The days of seeing the world in terms of isolated atoms are numbered. The emerging worldview proclaims the primacy of relationship over individuality. Though the philosopher Alfred North Whitehead speaks of religion as what an individual does with her or his solitariness, the solitariness of individual spiritual experience is itself a creative synthesis of countless conscious and unconscious influences on the emerging self. Our thoughts, prayers, and images contribute to a healing field of energy that enables another person or group to find wholeness, peace, and patience with what cannot be changed, as well as to experience profound emotional, physical, or spiritual transformation.

Taking your medicine in a holy way
Jesus integrated the use of saliva, mud, and faith in the healing of the deaf and blind. This was not unusual, since the use of saliva and mud poultices were a component of conventional medical care in the ancient world. One healing narrative describes Jesus making a poultice with mud and saliva and applying it to the eyes of a man blind from birth. Yet his use of a common first-century medical remedy was *preceded* by a theological discourse absolving the man and

his parents from responsibility for his blindness and it was *followed* by the command to go to the pool of Siloam to cleanse his eyes (John 9:1–7). The "natural" remedy became a vehicle of grace and forgiveness.

Today, followers of the healing path of Jesus can similarly join prayer with their morning medications, or meditation with chemotherapy or radiation sessions. Jesus' ministry demonstrates that there is no wall of separation between faith and medicine. God's desire for physical wholeness is worked out just as effectively through Western and complementary medicine as it is through intercessory prayer and the laying on of hands. God uses science as well as spirituality to promote well-being and to respond to sickness. Jesus recognized that healing of the spirit contributes to physical well-being. He also affirmed that physical and social healing can also transform persons' *spiritual* lives.

Healing is gradual as well as dramatic

Today, many persons expect instant answers and dramatic healings from medical and spiritual interventions. We are an "instant gratification" society. While televangelists promise immediate healings to those who attend their services, follow-up research has shown that, in reality, many of the healings involve only temporary relief of pain or limitation through the placebo effect or faith factor, or have already involved a prior process of personal and intercessory prayers and medical care.

While we do not deny the possibility of instant healings or the channeling of divine power by televangelists and spiritual healers, we suspect that most healings of body, mind, and spirit reflect the fulfillment of an ongoing process, involving the regular practice of prayer as well as the active and compassionate prayerful support of a community. Most long-term healings of mind, body, and spirit reflect an interplay of the divinely grounded aim of healing already resident in our immune systems, emotions, and mental and physical resources; and our basic openness to the inflow of divine energy through prayer, meditation, imagination, medical care, healing arts such as reiki, and personal faith.

We must remember that, from time to time, Jesus himself had to be patient with the healing process. According to one gospel account, Jesus recognized the necessity of a gradual healing process when he healed a blind man at Bethsaida.

> *He took the blind man by the hand and led him out of the village; and when he put saliva on his eyes and laid his hands on him, he asked him, "Can you see anything?" And the man looked up and said, "I can see people, but they look like trees, walking." Then Jesus laid his hands on his eyes again; and he looked intently and his sight was restored, and he saw clearly. Then he sent him away to his home, saying, "Do not even go into the village."*
>
> Mark 8:22–26

gradual

The healing process, even among persons of great faith, can be gradual in nature. While God's will is always for abundant life and wholeness, often the healing we need does not occur until we are ready to receive it. Some persons never receive the cure they seek, but still may find an unexpected healing that enables them to respond creatively to chronic or terminal illness.

Reality is multi-factorial. Health and illness cannot be reduced to a glib religious formula, spiritual practice, or self-help book. Nor can we assume that there is a linear relationship between our faith and physical condition, or even God's will and the healing process. In a relational and ecological universe, our well-being is shaped by countless factors, far beyond our personal faith or unfaith. Some of these factors – such as family; social influences; our attitudes toward ourselves and others; our personal faith, spiritual practices, current physical condition, and genetics – may slow down the healing process or block it entirely. Still, God's intention is for wholeness and the energy of love still flows. As we open to God's spirit by joining prayer, worship, and healing practices such as reiki, new energies are released which may open the channels of healing. Even when a physical cure cannot be achieved, a healing of the spirit is always possible.

The healing power of a safe place

Jesus admonishes the man cured of blindness to return home without even entering the village. The village is not yet a safe place for this recently healed man. People's negative expectations may bring him down and set back his long-term healing adventure. The demon-possessed man of the Gerasenes wishes to follow Jesus, but is told to return home and let his life be an example in his familiar environment. The naysayers are not permitted to enter the place where Jairus' daughter is lying comatose. Her healing depends on the power of affirmative faith, embodied by Jesus, his closest disciples, and her parents.

Healing often requires a safe and familiar place. Our task as members of healing communities is to create circles of safety, where persons in pain can experience comfort, wholeness, and relief. In circles of compassionate love, the chaos and vulnerability arising from illness, stress, abuse, and fear find sanctuary and peace.

Jesus often sent people home to let their healings sink in. Too much public activity, like the premature use of broken leg or sprained wrist, may put our newfound healing at risk. God's work is often subtle and may take months and years to reach fulfillment in our lives. In the meantime, the gentle process of healing requires constancy of care and confidence in one's safety and security when one is most vulnerable. Regular times of reiki and communal prayer often provide "touchstones" that remind us that even when we are unaware of it, the healing process is at work in our lives.

THE CIRCLE OF HEALING

God's energy of love is boundless and all-inclusive. God's loving care addresses every need, bringing balance, wholeness, and vitality to body as well as spirit. The gospels do not present an exhaustive account of Jesus' healing ministry. Rather, they report the healings that most definitively reflected the interplay between divine compassion and human need in Jesus' time. Wherever there was a need, Jesus sought to respond to it. Abundant in his love, Jesus believed that all moments are *kairos* moments, that any time is the right time for healing. All places are "thin" places; all days are holy days. Though Jesus, like his Jewish companions, observed the Sabbath, he recognized that religious rituals and doctrines are always subservient to human needs. The deepest rest of the Sabbath arises from enabling others, wherever and whenever we encounter them, to more fully experience God's presence in their lives.

Always open to the presence of God in the least among us, Jesus healed and empowered persons with all types of physical and mental illness, and, in so doing, transformed their place in the social order. Jesus was also a friend of his society's marginalized and forgotten members. Social outcasts, defined solely by physical conditions such as leprosy, found a place of refuge, hospitality, and healing in Jesus' touch and welcome.

Jesus responded to the deepest needs of persons with impairments in vision, hearing, and speech, as well as to persons with paralysis and palsy. He invited people who were dominated by sin and guilt to receive the forgiveness that would enable them to start their lives all over again.

In times of transition and social dislocation, people are more susceptible to the "inner demons" of mental illness. These illnesses may have been due primarily to stress, epileptic seizures, inability to cope with change, childhood abuse, anxiety, or chemical imbalances. But no matter what the cause, Jesus sought to call forth the "higher" or "healthy" self of each person he encountered. To those who suffered from the loss of the centered self, Jesus brought the hope of restoration and of return to normalcy and centeredness.

The greatest enemy, however, is death. Despite advances in medical care, the mortality rate remains at 100 percent. Eventually, all of us will have to face our own death and the deaths of loved ones. Bruce often reminded his medical students at Georgetown University School of Medicine that "everyone you treat will eventually die; just hope it's not on your watch!"

All of the persons Jesus healed eventually died. Their deaths remind us that the ultimate goal of healing is an intimate and trusting relationship with God, and not merely

physical health and longevity. Although the primary focus of
Jesus' healing mission centered on the living rather than the
dead, he also awakened Lazarus, and the widow of Nain's son,
from the sleep of the dead. While the idea of raising the dead
apart from medical technology pushes the rational mind to its
limits, it is clear that in both cases Jesus' primary motivation
was to respond to the needs of those who depended on the
deceased for their economic and relational well-being.

Jesus himself was the recipient of the greatest healing
miracle – the Resurrection. While the Resurrection will always remain a mystery to the faithful and a scandal to the
rationalist, Jesus' spiritually lively resurrection body is the
vehicle for new life for those who face death in its many
forms. From the mystery of Easter, a community of salvation
and healing arose. Broken hearts found healing and fearful
spirits found courage. Two thousand years later, the mystery
of the Resurrection still gives us hope that we can creatively
face our own mortality and the deaths of loved ones. Our
death is part of a larger journey of companionship with the
God of healing and love.

The impact of Jesus' healings live on in the 21st century.
His healings continue to shape our lives. Christ is alive! As
teacher, mentor, healer, and savior, Jesus charged his followers
with a ministry of healing, in which he promised that they
could do even greater works of healing and transformation
than his own. He empowered his own disciples to be vehicles
of God's healing touch by the laying on of hands and by the
sharing of the divine spirit. In the words of Luke's gospel,

> Then Jesus called the twelve together and gave
> them power and authority over all demons and
> to cure diseases, and he sent them out to proclaim

*the kingdom of God and to heal... They departed
and went through the villages, bringing the good
news and curing diseases everywhere.*
Luke 9:1–2, 6

As he prepared to depart from this world, Jesus called his disciples to be the pioneers of an adventure of healing and wholeness. In John's gospel, Jesus breathes on them and thus attunes them to a higher spiritual energy, whose power will flow through them from now on.

*And Jesus said to them again, "Peace be with
you. As God sent me, so I send you." When he
had said this, he breathed on them and said,
"Receive the Holy Spirit."*
John 20:21–22

Initiation into this holy adventure was completed on Pentecost, when the followers of Jesus, both male and female, were engulfed by a mighty wind and enlivened by tongues of fire, giving them the power to preach, teach, and heal (Acts 2:1–4). Today, the spirit still blows and the energy of love still enlivens, calling us to become healers in our own time and in accordance with the medical, theological, and psychological insights of our world.

As one of the many spiritual practices, rituals, and healing techniques that enable followers of Jesus to share the good news, reiki healing touch uniquely embodies the warmth of the Spirit and the breath of life. Reiki's gentle touch passes the Healing Spirit from one person to the next, through the unbounded grace of God. Through the healing touch of reiki, God's light still shines to bring healing to individuals and communities.

3

OPENING TO
THE ENERGY OF LOVE

An argument arose among them as to which one of them was the greatest. But Jesus, aware of their inner thoughts, took a little child and put it by his side, and said to them, "Whoever welcomes this child in my name welcomes me, and whoever welcomes me welcomes the one who sent me; for the least among all of you is the greatest."

John answered, "Master, we saw someone casting out demons in your name, and we tried to stop him, because he does not follow with us." But Jesus said to him, "Do not stop him; because whoever is not against you is for you."

Luke 9:46–50

One day, while he was teaching, Pharisees and teachers of the law were sitting nearby (they had come from every village of Galilee and Judea and from Jerusalem); and the power of the Lord was with him to heal.

Luke 5:17

Reiki opens us to the divine healing energy flowing through all things. This energy of love, which flows from within as well as beyond us, is a manifestation of God's transforming power in our lives. This energy of love is universal. It is not bound by creed, ritual, or faith tradition. This spiritual energy, known as *chi* in Chinese spirituality and medicine, and as *ki* in the Japanese culture from which reiki arose, and as *prana* in Hindu Ayurvedic medicine, is the source of health and wholeness in its many forms.

While the Hebraic and Christian traditions did not formulate a philosophy of medicine or a theory of healing energy, the energy, whose working is described with terms such as *chi, prana, chakras, auras,* and *meridians* may be identified with the Christian and Hebraic images of *pneuma,* the spiritual life force in all things; *ruach,* the breath of life; and the dynamic power and energy that flowed forth from Jesus' spiritual center and healing hands.

Agnes Sanford, who pioneered healing ministries within the Episcopal church and mainline Christianity, affirms that

> *God is within us and without us. He [sic] is the source of all life; and of unimaginable depths of inter-stellar space. He is also the indwelling life of our own little selves. And just as the whole world full of electricity will not light a house unless the house itself is prepared to receive that energy, so the infinite and eternal God cannot help us unless we are prepared to receive the light within ourselves.*[1]

Divine life pulses through all things, giving birth to solar systems and zygotes, mystical experiences and the quest for justice. Long before the rise of quantum physics and the popularity of energy work in the Western world, John's gospel proclaimed that "all things came into being through [the light of the world] and without it nothing came into being. What has come into being with [the light] was life, and the life was the light of all people" (John 1:3–4). Could this light have been the energy that brought forth the big bang and that continues to give life and direction to cosmic evolution? To those of us who affirm the lively presence of God in all things, the answer is clearly, "Yes!"

Today, medical science is recognizing that health and disease are dynamic, relational processes, rather than static, linear events. While there is no one ideal form of wholeness, our own unique well-being arises from the interplay of factors such as our attitudes, spiritual life and core values, relationships, family of origin, social environment, diet, physical environment, education, economic situation, genetic makeup, lifestyle, and age. Each factor shapes the dynamic process of health, even though at certain times one particular factor may predominate. This multi-factorial vision of health liberates us from guilt, on the one hand, but also challenges us to participate in personal and social transformation, on the other. We are not the omnipotent masters of our destiny, creating our own reality in its entirety by our thoughts and attitudes. But we are also not the passive victims of our environment, genetics, and family of origin. Our choice to pursue spiritual growth, positive attitudes, a healthy lifestyle, and authentic relationships may be a significant factor in enhancing our health. Accordingly, although God's aim for our lives is always toward wholeness and health, we must align our lives with this divine creativity and abundance, rather than turn away from the God of healing.

In chapter one, we reflected on Jesus' image of the vine and branches. Connected to the vine, we bear much fruit. Severed from the vine, we wither physically and spiritually. When the energy of love flows through us without obstruction, we experience health and wholeness of body, mind, and spirit, and face illness with hope and creativity. When that energy is blocked or imbalanced due to environmental disease, personal choices, spiritual neglect, genetics, or other factors, we are susceptible to diseases of the body, mind, and spirit.

In reflecting on our role in health and illness, Sanford comments that

> *when we establish a closer connection with God in prayer, we should receive more abundant life – an increased flow of energy. The creative force that sustains us is increased within our bodies.*[2]

Our openness to God does not insure perfect well-being or the cure of disease, but it enables us to experience wholeness even when we face chronic illnesses of mind, body, and spirit.

I have quoted Agnes Sanford at length in this section because her pioneering healing ministry, conducted within mainstream Protestantism, makes possible a partnership between reiki healing and mainstream Christianity. While many traditional Christians worry about the invocation of words such as healing energy, energy centers, or chi, prana, chakras, or auric fields by certain healing energy workers and spiritual healers within the Christian community, Sanford's interpretation of Jesus' ministry invites us to expand our vision of healing and wholeness. In contrast to those who would limit Jesus' healing ministry to a few self-identified protectors of theological, spiritual, or liturgical orthodoxy, the Healing Jesus proclaimed that anyone who heals in the name of Christ is doing God's work. In the quest for health and healing, "whoever is not against you is for you" (Luke 9:50).

A church with a vital, growing healing ministry will embrace the many gifts of God's children, whether they are innovative, exotic, or traditional. Reiki healing is one of the many ways we can open ourselves to God's healing energy for the well-being of others and ourselves. Unique in its simplicity as a prayer form, reiki simply relies upon God's grace rather than on manipulation of our energy or consciousness.

In the following pages, we will describe the reiki training program that we facilitate throughout the country. We share our own approach as one model for reiki training with congregations or ecumenical Christian groups. Our approach to reiki training is intended to equip followers of Jesus to be greater channels of healing in their communities of faith.

HANDS OF LIGHT

At a reiki training workshop in Bethesda, Maryland, Sondra exclaimed, "My hands are tingling. I feel heat and power flow through them." As she gave her first reiki treatment, her healing partner Marie exclaimed, "I can't believe it. Wherever she touches me, I feel warmth and peace." After 15 minutes of receiving a reiki treatment, Marie affirmed, "I haven't felt so relaxed in months. Usually, I'm so wound up that I can barely sit still. This is a miracle!"

Kevin came to the reiki training in St. Mary's, Pennsylvania, with the beginning of a migraine headache. The pain was so intense that he barely made it through the introductory lecture. But when Bruce touched his head during the first reiki attunement, he felt energy course through his whole body. "At that moment, I forgot all about my headache. The energy seemed to soothe and wash it away. I felt no pain the rest of the day. Now, whenever I feel the first signs of a migraine, I close my eyes, breathe deeply, and give myself a reiki treatment. And the pain either goes away or becomes more manageable."

Analytic by nature and profession, Rosemary came to her first reiki training event with a great deal of skepticism. As she introduced herself around the circle, she warned us in advance, "I'm not sure what to expect or if anything's going to happen today. I want evidence, something I can experience. But I'm willing to be open-minded." Five hours later, Rosemary confessed, "I was skeptical when I came here today. But I've felt the energy flow through my hands, and my partner said she felt warmth and healing in my hands. I even felt the energy when my partner gave me a treatment. I'm still not certain what's going on with reiki healing, but now I believe that I can make a difference with my hands. I can help people feel better. And that's good enough for me!"

The experience of these reiki practitioners echoes Agnes Sanford's description of a healing encounter with a child that she treated with prayer and laying on of hands.

> *I went to see a little girl who had been in a cast*
> *for five months following infantile paralysis. One*

day I placed my hands above the rigid knee in that instinctive laying on of hands that every mother knows... And I asked that the light of God might shine through me into that small, stiff knee and make it well.

"Oh, take your hands away!" cried the little girl. "It's hot."

"That's God's power working in your knee, Sally," I replied. "It's like electricity working in your lamp. I guess it has to be hot, so as to make your knee come back to life."[3]

While no one fully knows the answer to that little girl's question, reiki is a simple and easy-to-learn way to turn on the divine electricity in our hands. The practice of reiki changes lives. Reiki healing touch enables us to awaken to God's healing energy and to gracefully let it flow through us to bring wholeness to others. Although God's healing touch is available everywhere, reiki cleanses and balances the divine energy within our lives and enables us to be more effective channels of that energy to others. In the spirit of Jesus' story of the vine and branches, reiki connects us with the abundant sap of the vine and allows us to bear the fruits of healing and transformation. All we need to do is to open to God's healing energy and care-fully touch one another in love.

But how do you give a reiki treatment and how can you access with greater abundance the divine power that permeates us at all times? In this section, we will give a close-up view of a reiki training session, describe the mechanics of reiki, and explore the various levels of reiki healing. While reiki cannot be taught on paper, I hope that the following "snapshots" from a reiki workshop will inspire you to consider integrating reiki into your spiritual life or, if you are already practicing or teaching reiki, support your own healing journey and enable you to make clear connections between reiki and your Christian faith.

A brand new day

At 9:00 a.m., a group of friends and strangers are gathering in our healing room in Potomac, Maryland, shaking hands, exchanging greetings, and getting to know one another. Laughter and friendship fill the air. There is also a pervasive sense of anticipation and adventure. Each of the participants is here for a deeper purpose – to experience God's healing light in her or his life. Like St. Francis of Assisi, each one desires to be a more effective instrument of God's peace in her or his family and church. Each participant yearns to bring God's healing touch to her or his workplace, home, church, or loved ones. The participants come with great expectations and these expectations will be fulfilled by the end of the workshop. By the end of the day, they will experience the energy of love in a new way. Learning the first level of reiki healing touch will change their lives forever. They will open in unexpected and powerful ways to the divine energy that brings healing and growth.

The day begins with a moment of prayer and affirmation: "O God of healing light. Send forth your healing touch upon us. Touch us with light, love, and healing. We open to your healing energy. Let it flow through us that we might be blessed to be a blessing to others. In Jesus' name. Amen."

After going around the circle with introductions and a sharing of hopes, we ask the group to take a few minutes for a centering prayer. We invite them to close their eyes, breathe gently, and let go of the worries of the day. After

REIKI HEALING TOUCH ✳ 67

they are relaxed, we ask them to breathe in God's healing light – "the light of the world, the light of Christ, in whom we live, move, and have our being." In the meditation, the participants experience their whole being in terms of God's light. Divine light cleanses and vitalizes each person's mind, body, and spirit. We conclude with a brief prayer of affirmation, simply asking God to bless this day and our lives. As teachers, we seek to create an environment of acceptance, affirmation, and surprise in which students feel comfortable taking risks and claiming the novelty and openness of the "beginner's mind."

The morning continues with a brief lecture on the history of reiki and its relationship to the current state of Western and complementary medicine, with plenty of time set aside for questions and comments. We typically reflect on the growing partnership of spirituality and medicine, the research on the benefits of spiritual life and religious commitment on health, and the fact that reiki practitioners are adventurers in a new world of spirituality and health. Then we briefly discuss the unique nature of reiki healing, the universal energy flowing through all things, and give the participants a description of the day ahead. Before we take a break, we share the stories of reiki's origins and remind the students that, despite the challenges of constructing an accurate biography of Usui and his first students, Usui and his followers are archetypal figures in the quest for global healing that joins East and West.

Tuning in to the energy of love

The heart of reiki is found in reiki attunements or initiation rituals. Due to the hands-on and personal nature of the reiki attunements, we cannot describe the attunements in any detail. In fact, they can only be rightly passed on from master-teacher to student. Nevertheless, the purpose of the attunements is to open, cleanse, and transform the personal energy of the reiki student. Using an analogy from gardening: while once the energy may have flowed through the student with the intensity and strength of a garden hose, following the first attunement, it will flow through her or him with the power and focus of a fire hose!

The ritual touching, breath, and use of the reiki symbols by a reiki teacher in the attunements awakens the divine healing power within the student from that time on. From now on, just the intention to share reiki healing touch will activate the lively flow of reiki healing energy through the student's hands. Using Jesus' image of the vine and branches, we affirm that the healing energy is always flowing through our lives. The reiki attunements are simply one way of opening to a greater flow of God's energy in our lives, to enhance our own spiritual fruitfulness and the spiritual fruitfulness of others.

In preparing the students for the attunements, we invite them to enter a prayerful state. Since we feel strongly that persons should not be touched or manipulated without warning or permission, we tell the students in advance where we will touch them in the attunement process. In the graceful spirit of reiki, we invite the students to be open to whatever emerges in the course of the attunements. We also remind them that experiencing sensations of heat and light are common, but not at all necessary for being an effective channel of divine healing. We remind participants that, as Jesus' parable of the mustard seed illustrates, the most important growth is often gentle and undramatic.

As a way of reminding the students that reiki is not a

matter of effort or even of perception, Bruce reveals that he didn't feel anything for months following his level one course, and, in fact, felt like a failure. "So if I can learn reiki," he playfully assures them, "anyone can!"

During the four attunements of level one reiki, some students have brief mystical experiences (they see a light or experience Christ's presence in an intimate way), while others feel a dramatic unblocking of energy, similar to the impact of an acupuncture treatment. The vast majority of the students, however, experience the attunements as gentle, peaceful, and energizing. As they return to the meeting room after their first attunements, participants often feel an unusual but quite pleasant tingling in their hands.

As the group gathers once again, we lead them in a gentle time of centering. In the spirit of the Quakers, we invite them to experience the inner light of God as their deepest reality. We remind them that God's healing light is flowing through them and from now on they can consciously share the light of God with others. This segment of the class concludes with reflections on their experience of receiving the first attunement.

Following the break, we talk about the relationship between Christian faith and reiki healing. Grounded in the affirmation that "wherever truth and healing is present, God is its source," we describe areas of continuity between reiki healing touch, the laying on of hands, and the healing ministry of Jesus. We root reiki solidly in the Christian understanding of God's presence in the world, its convergence with the emerging worldview of the new physics, and the growing evidence of the "faith factor" in health and healing. We also draw parallels between reiki and other complementary health modalities. Our goal is for the students to integrate

reiki into their lives as followers of Jesus who are committed to the healing of themselves and others. We invite them
to see reiki as an essential part of their own devotional life
and commitment to service.

Following the lecture, level one students receive a second
attunement. As we gather following the attunement, we once
again ask the students to share their experiences or any
questions they might have. Typically, following this question
and answer period, we break for an "agape" lunch, a time of
joyful sharing for healing partners.

Touching holiness. After lunch, we demonstrate the basic
hands-on reiki positions. While we remind the students
that there is no one way to give a reiki treatment, there are
certain patterns and practices that particularly support the
healing of yourself and those you treat with reiki. Similar
to the sacraments of the Christian church, reiki brings
wholeness regardless of the state of mind of the practitioner
or the person receiving the treatment. However, we affirm
the importance of nurturing a sanctuary for your reiki by
adhering to the following healthy behaviors:

1. creating a hospitable environment for those who come
   for reiki treatments,
2. keeping a peaceful state of mind as a practitioner,
3. following a consistent order of treatment with each person
   for the purpose of establishing a sense of confidence and
   trust (for example, although a treatment may begin at the
   head or the midsection, during a formal reiki session it
   is important to begin at the same place throughout your
   reiki relationship),
4. maintaining appropriate professional boundaries and
   confidentiality,

5. taking care of your own spiritual and physical well-being, and

6. participating in spiritual friendships or peer groups with other reiki practitioners.

Last but not least, a healing sanctuary is guided by the affirmation that the healing relationship is "not about you," but focuses on the healing and wholeness of the recipient of reiki healing touch. This implies checking in regularly about their comfort and concerns at the beginning and throughout the treatment.

In applying the reiki healing touch positions, it is not only important to be consistent in the order of the hand positions, but also to cover as much of the body as possible within the parameters of the basic positions. While the focus of the treatment is the organs and energy centers, we suggest that practitioners also focus on the knees and the soles of feet in order to ground the healing energy. A traditional reiki treatment takes between 45 minutes and an hour. However, if you have only a few minutes, gently touching a certain injured part of the body brings comfort and healing.

Reiki always centers on the well-being of the one who is treated, not on the practitioner's convenience, pleasure, or self-aggrandizement. Reiki challenges the practitioner to cultivate a sense of spiritual stature, which sees the well-being of the receiver and practitioner as intimately connected.

Reiki "laying on of hands" is applied to the body surface palms down, and does not require the receiver to change clothes or disrobe. It may be applied through clothing, blankets, casts, or bandages. Any part of the body may be treated, but before beginning, the practitioner asks a few simple questions to guide her or his treatment:

- How are you feeling?
- How would you describe your overall health of body, mind, and spirit?
- Are there any places of discomfort or injury upon which you would particularly like me to lay my hands?
- Are there any places that you would particularly like me *not* to lay my hands?

If the person receiving a reiki treatment has a serious medical condition, the practitioner asks about the nature of their current medical treatment and may request authorization from their primary care physician. Reiki always complements the receivers' medical treatment and affirms the expertise of physicians and other trained complementary health care givers.

Reiki involves sensitivity to the other's personal energy; it also involves a willingness to listen and to respond without judgment to the words and feelings of the other. As a form of healing touch, reiki honors the integrity and personal space of those who receive treatments. Reiki practitioners commit themselves to use their lives and their hands for healing and love. If the receiver prefers not to have a part of the body touched that would normally be done as part of a standard reiki treatment, the practitioner simply gives the treatment three or four inches above that spot, within the energy field of the person. In this way, reiki can be applied in a way similar to the modalities of therapeutic and healing touch. Reiki brings health and wholeness, whether we touch the recipient's body directly or minister to her or his energy fields.

In preparation for their first experiences as reiki practitioners, we remind students of the importance of their own comfort while giving a reiki treatment. No two receivers or practitioners are alike and it is important to adjust the reiki treatment to the size of the receiver as well as to your own stature and physical condition. Healthy practitioners enhance the flow of this graceful energy by paying mindful attention to their body mechanics, and to their spiritual and mental state of being. Whether you sit or stand while giving a treatment, the key is to find comfortable position. It is important to adjust the height of the massage or reiki table to the size of the recipient and to the height of the reiki practitioner. The practitioner's fatigue, back pain, failure to eat or drink before a treatment, or own inner chaos, may detract from an otherwise positive experience for both giver and receiver. In the same way, a cluttered space or a chaotic environment detracts from the peace and comfort that the receiver seeks in the treatment process.

The example of the sacraments is helpful here. Sacraments, such as Holy Communion, ultimately mediate God's grace regardless of the environment or spiritual condition of the pastor. But the physical maintenance of the sanctuary, the spiritual integrity and openness of the pastor, and the spiritual commitment of the participants shape our experience of the sacraments, if not the overall efficacy of the sacrament to mediate that grace to our lives. In a similar fashion, the temperature of the room, low lighting, gentle music, and candles, along with the spiritual centeredness of the practitioner, add to the well-being of both the recipient and the practitioner.

In the practice of reiki, as in all spiritual leadership, caring for another is intimately related to caring for ourselves. As the practitioner nurtures her or his own spiritual life and attends to her or his overall physical and spiritual health, the recipient experiences greater centeredness, care, and wholeness. In the words of Mother Teresa, in reiki we are simply trying to do "something beautiful for God."

After this introduction to the practical considerations of giving reiki treatments, the students practice by giving each other treatments. Often, for the first time in their lives, students experience themselves as channels of blessing and healing. They soon discover that they can enhance their experience of the flow of energy by keeping their fingers and hands together, by breathing deeply and mindfully, and by focusing on the intention to be a healing companion.

Following the treatments, we gather for questions and comments, and then give the third attunement. Students often comment in amazement about the heat in their hands or how peaceful it was to give or receive a treatment.

Following the third attunement, the group gathers for one last time to focus in greater detail on the ethics of reiki and the spirituality of the practitioner. In reiki, the practitioner and the practice are united. Personal integrity is essential to the practice of reiki. In the final chapter, we discuss in greater detail the spiritual practices of the reiki path, which include commitment to personal spiritual disciplines, self-reiki, care for the body and mind, ethical accountability and peer support, and service. Self-care is an issue of character as well as self-affirmation. To promote their own well-being, we always suggest that students give themselves regular reiki treatments, beginning with the head and going to the pelvis.

Because reiki is a matter of character and spiritual priorities, we discuss the ethical principles of reiki and the commitment of each practitioner to a life of gratitude, peace, community service, and healing. We believe that it should be the intent of every reiki practitioner to use their hands of light only for reconciliation, love, and service.

Just as in other hands-on healing techniques such as massage, therapeutic touch, and healing touch, it is essential in reiki to respect the integrity of the receiver. Reiki practitioners observe the highest ethical standards in terms of boundaries, touch, and confidentiality. While reiki and its application can be sensual, it is never sexual in nature. In the practice of reiki, Jesus' ministry of compassion and care is our ultimate model. Those who practice reiki commit themselves to becoming healers "in Christ's place" – loving their neighbors with the same care as they love themselves.

Following a time of questions and comments, students are given the fourth and final level one attunement.

Walking in the light of God

As the day ends, the class discusses reiki levels two and three. We talk about reiki as a way of life in which we are conscious bearers of Christ's healing touch, able to bring wholeness to every situation. While we cannot predict or control the flow of divine energy or assume dramatic effects from our healing touch, we can have confidence that from now on we will be a healing presence in every situation.

Usually, our workshop concludes with a meditation on God's ever-flowing light and love, which affirms that this healing light will be the student's companion, helper, and guide from now on. In reiki level one, we discover that God's universal energy constantly flows through us and that we are God's partners in sharing that healing energy with others. Our practice of reiki enables us to join our own healing with the healing of the planet.

REIKI LEVEL TWO:
A JOURNEY WITHOUT DISTANCE

At a reiki two workshop, students learn the role of the traditional reiki symbols in focusing and expanding the energy of love that flows through them. According to many students of religious experience, religious symbols participate in a reality deeper than everyday consciousness and mediate the infinite power of the universe to finite situations. This is true for reiki symbols as well. While we do not fully know the origins of these symbols, they are rooted in the healing experiences of Tibetan Buddhists, as revealed to Mikao Usui.

In a reiki two workshop, the primary focus is on enhancing our experience of the nature of divine power in our lives, by learning to use the reiki symbols for healing at a distance, increasing mental and spiritual harmony, and focusing and expanding healing energy. Similar to level one, the level two workshop involves further attunements, along with instruction in three reiki symbols and their meaning and use.

At a level two workshop, I remind participants that the practice of distant healing as a form of intercessory prayer is essential to Christian spirituality and healing. Jesus healed persons by touching, teaching, and welcoming. He also healed persons at a distance. Neither time nor space, nor social standing nor ethnicity limited Jesus' compassionate love, and neither should it limit our own Christian compassion.

One of most remarkable findings of contemporary physics helps us understand the nature of intercessory prayer and distant healing. This principle is called "non-local causation." According to physicist John Stewart Bell, if distant objects have once been in contact, a change in one elicits a change in the other – no matter how far apart they are, even if they are at opposite ends of the universe. Physician Larry Dossey affirms that non-locality may even apply to the mind. Consciousness itself, Dossey asserts, is non-local in nature. Our thoughts and feelings radiate across the universe.

While the biblical tradition makes no mention of the intricacies of energy fields, chakras, physics, or speculative cosmology, it nevertheless gives evidence to the reality of non-local influences that suggest that the energy of love flows without regard to distance. Jesus' healing of the Syrophoenician woman's daughter and the centurion's servant, as well as the practice of intercessory prayer in the early church, point to a spiritual ecology that transcends the usual boundaries of time or space.

The body of Christ, which not only relates to the community of faith but also to the essential nature of Christ-filled reality, manifests this same tightly woven unity of experience. What happens to one member shapes the experience and quality of life of all the others. Further, the practice of intercessory prayer is grounded in the vision of a dynamic and relational universe in which our prayers create a field of healing energy around others and support God's aim of wholeness in all things. In speaking of prayer, Larry Dossey notes the following:

> If prayer were a conventional form of energy, it should weaken as distance is increased, and this does not happen. If it were energy, its effects could be shielded, but this has not proved possible. This strongly suggests that prayer does not involve any conventional form of energy or signal, that it does not travel from here to there, and that it may not "go" anywhere at all.

If prayer does not go anywhere, then it may be simultaneously present everywhere, enveloping sender, object, and the Almighty all at once.[4]

Dossey believes, and we agree, that the often-used term "sending energy" is a metaphor for our individual participation and contribution to the universal and omnipresent energy of God.

In level two of reiki training, the practitioner learns to be a conscious channel for distant or non-local healing. Non-local or distant reiki is simply a prayer form, employing certain symbols and the imaginative visualization of a person or situation, in order to focus and enhance the healing energy of the universe for another person, a past or future event, or ourselves. We believe that distant reiki is a type of inter-cessory prayer that can be creatively integrated with any traditional Christian healing and devotional practice. The symbols used in level two reiki center our minds, invoke our experience of the divine, and surround others with love, in the same way that the liturgical gestures at Communion or the sign of the cross mediate and enhance our experience of God's presence. Distant reiki connects us with others and the love of God in a healing and loving fashion.

In level two reiki, students also learn to enhance their own personal energy and to create a healing environment for themselves and others. For Christians, practicing the lessons of level two reiki means putting into action the basic affirmation of Philippians 4:13:"I can do all things through Christ who strengthens me." As God's partners in creativity and healing, we have the power to do great things and to transform the world. In reiki two, the energy that flowed vi-brantly as a result of the level one attunements now expands both in its intensity and focus.

Healing energy involves not only intensity but also clarity, integrity, and wisdom. In level two reiki training, students learn a symbol whose purpose, when applied to the forehead or the top of the head, is to bring harmony and balance to our spiritual lives. This healing symbol joins the spirit within us with God's "sighs too deep" for words, as it aligns us with God's highest good for our lives and for those for whom we pray. Christian reiki practice assumes that each one of us possesses the light of Christ as our deepest reality. Though often forgotten, this inner Christ gives us the wisdom, inspiration, courage, and strength we need to bless others and to experience God's blessing in our lives.

In reiki two, we learn to unblock the impediments to our spiritual growth and ability to mediate healing energy for the spiritual well-being of others. Ancient wounds are healed and present anxiety is calmed. Operating at the deepest level of our being, these reiki symbols enable the energies of spiritual and emotional healing to flow with greater intensity and purity as they cleanse both our conscious and unconscious experience, so that we might become clearer channels of God's grace.

BLESSED TO BE A BLESSING

The practice of reiki joins our well-being with the healing of the world. In level three reiki training, those persons who are called to a deeper healing ministry experience new dimensions of God's healing energy and learn to enable others to experience more fully the light of healing in their lives. Briefly put, level three, or the reiki teaching level, involves a lengthy journey of spiritual discernment, practical application, and holy apprenticeship under the guidance of a spiritual mentor and teacher. In many ways, level three reiki uniquely combines the inner journey of spiritual formation with the outer journey of service.

Becoming a master teacher involves deepening your spiritual life and examining your own motivations and places of brokenness so that they may become openings for the healing of others. The gift of reiki teaching challenges us to become not so much "wounded healers" as "healed healers," that is, Christian servants committed to the highest spiritual values, to lives of integrity, and to promoting the well-being of others. A reiki teacher must make a conscious decision to walk the path of reiki spiritual values through self-care and spiritual development, intellectual growth, character formation, service, and an ongoing commitment to being an instrument of peace and healing. If he or she is involved in a community of faith, a reiki master teacher may be called to a ministry of healing within the church, which involves giving both hands-on and distant reiki treatments, teaching reiki to fellow congregants, and serving "the least of these."

At every level of reiki, ultimately the goal is the same – to become an open and effective channel of healing and blessing through sharing the light of God with others.

4

THE WISDOM
OF THE BODY

Now there are varieties of gifts, but the same Spirit; and there are a variety of services, but the same Lord; and there are varieties of activities, but it is the same God who activates all of them in everyone. To each is given the manifestation of the Spirit for the common good. To one is given through the Spirit the utterance of wisdom, and to another the utterance of knowledge according to the same Spirit, to another faith by the same Spirit, to another gifts of healing by the one Spirit, to another the working of miracles, to another prophecy, to another the discernment of spirits, to another various kinds of tongues, to another the interpretation of tongues. All these are activated by one and the same Spirit, who allots to each one individually just as the Spirit chooses.

For just as the body is one and has many members, and all the members of the body, though many, are one body, so it is with Christ...

If one member suffers, all suffer together with it; if one member is honored, all rejoice together with it. Now you are the body of Christ, and individually members of it.

1 Corinthians 12:4–12, 26–27

The energy of love flows through all things, giving birth to whole persons and healthy communities, and creating an ecology of healing in which each part shapes the well-being of the totality. Divine energy animates and guides all things, bringing forth communities and persons who are particularly attentive to the flow of the Spirit. This attentiveness arises from the dynamic interplay of divine inspiration and human responsiveness.

Two thousand years ago, the apostle Paul described one such community of openness as the "body of Christ." Permeated by the lively energy of Christ, each member is ordered and joined to all the others through its own unique revelation of divine creativity. Holographic in nature, each part dynamically reflects the wisdom of the whole, even as the whole arises from the lively interplay of the parts.

Today, the church is rediscovering this interdependent vision of the "the body of Christ," in which each member reflects divine wisdom as its deepest identity. Inspired by the growing partnership of spirituality and medicine, the church is reclaiming the ancient gifts of healing, wholeness, and shalom. Followers of Jesus are once again discovering that the quest for healing is at the heart of the ministry and mission of the church. Awakened to its identity as the living, growing, interdependent body of Christ, the church calls forth the gifts of each member for the healing of people and the planet. While divine creativity manifests itself in many ways, each person is called to be a healer reflecting God's aim of abundant life.

The practice of reiki healing enables many Christians to embody God's goal of healing and wholeness. Awakened to God's universal energy, we can claim our diverse gifts as God's healing channels in whatever context we find ourselves. Yet the gift of reiki healing touch is often overlooked in the community of faith. Many reiki practitioners feel as if they must hide their healing light under a bushel basket. They worry that their healing touch will be misunderstood, or judged as unorthodox, heretical, or "New Age" by their fellow Christians.

Nevertheless, God is calling the church to embrace healing in its many dimensions, including reiki healing touch. We believe that the God who seeks healing and wholeness for all persons is calling Christian reiki practitioners to let their light shine. In the emerging healing ministry of the church, reiki complements and empowers traditional healing practices, such as anointing with oil and laying on of hands. The healing light of reiki gives energy and direction to the church's healing mission in our unique time. In this chapter, we will explore the place of reiki healing touch in the context of the church's calling to be a community of care and healing.

THE TOUCH THAT HEALS

And Jesus could do no deed of power [in Nazareth], except that he laid his hands on a few sick people and cured them.

Mark 6:5

Then one of the disciples struck the slave of the high priest and cut off his right ear...and [Jesus] touched his ear and healed him.

Luke 22:50–51

Touch can heal, welcome, and transform. While the energy of love flows through every part of our bodies, historically, the hands have been seen as a special medium of divine power. Joined with prayer and the intention to be a channel for God's grace, appropriate touch can play an essential role in the healing ministry of the church. The "Order for Healing for Congregational Use" of the United Church of Christ uses the following traditional prayer during the laying on of hands.

> *I/we lay my/our hands upon you, so may God grant you the powerful presence of the Holy Spirit. With infinite mercy, may God forgive your sins, release you from suffering, and restore you to health and strength. May God deliver you from all evil, preserve you in all goodness, and bring you to ever lasting life; through Jesus Christ our Savior. Amen.*

A more contemporary prayer for the laying on of hands affirms:

> *I/we lay hands upon you in the name of our Sovereign and Savior Jesus Christ, calling on Christ to uphold you and fill you with grace, that you may know the healing power of God's love. Amen.*[1]

As we lay hands on another person for healing, in light of God's intention for healing, we become channels of God's healing love and light. Reiki healing touch mediates that same healing power by conveying God's universal healing power from one person to another.

A curious passage describing the ministry of the apostle Paul challenges us to go beyond the laying on of hands to recognize that our intention to channel God's healing light and love can be carried by any compassionate touch.

> *God did extraordinary things through Paul, so that when the handkerchiefs or aprons that had touched his skin were brought to the sick, their diseases left them, and the evil spirits came out of them.*
>
> Acts 19:11–12

A person with no arms and hands can use her or his feet or head to direct God's healing light or love toward another. Even persons who are bed-bound can be mediums of blessing by touch, thought, word, and prayer. Those who see themselves as limited to only one modality of healing need to remember that Jesus healed by being touched, as well as by touching. Anything, from a word to a handkerchief, can be a medium of divine energy.

Traditionally, the laying on of hands has been joined with ritual anointing with oil. Historically, oil has been used by virtually every culture to soothe, comfort, and heal. Joined with prayers, anointing mediates the grace of God through the interplay of touch and oil. In the biblical tradition, to be anointed is to be blessed, empowered, and healed. Anointing and laying on of hands invite the recipient to let go of control and let God's unconditional and unmerited grace flow into her or his life.

The power of anointing with oil in the context of a healing community is described in the epistle of James.

Are any among you suffering? They should pray. Are any cheerful? They should sing songs of praise. Are any among you sick? They should call for the elders of the church and have them pray over them, anointing them with oil in the name of the Lord. The prayer of faith will save the sick, and the Lord will raise them up; and anyone who has committed sins will be forgiven. Therefore confess your sins to one other, and pray for one another, so that you may be healed. The prayer of the righteous is powerful and effective.

James 5:13–16

This passage reminds us to place God at the center of our lives, regardless of our condition. There are no prerequisites for seeking healing. Simply recognizing your need and bringing it to the community in hope and expectation opens us to unexpected releases of divine power. Although guilt, negativity, and fear may block divine energy and lead to illnesses of body, mind, and spirit, they can never fully impede God's love or the care of a healing community. God's healing touch is given to all persons, regardless of their faith or physical condition. Still, the interplay of faith and confession of sin enable us to identify and release all that blocks divine energy from flowing through our lives. As we touch one another in love, giving of the sign of the cross as we place oil on one another's foreheads, we affirm that God's touch is physical as well as spiritual, and that God moves through every healing modality.

The prayer of thanksgiving for the oil of anointing expresses the graceful universality of this ritual of blessing and wholeness.

Eternal God, you are the Sun of Righteousness, who rises with healing in your wings to put to flight all enemies that assault us. We thank you for oil, used by prophets and apostles as a sign of God's favor. Send your Holy Spirit on us and on this medicine of mercy that through this anointing your servants may again know the health that comes from you; through Jesus Christ our Savior. Amen.[2]

The church is challenged to create circles of healing whose hospitality invites persons to seek healing for themselves and for others. These healing circles embrace all who come for healing with a love that has no beginning or end. There is no one way to create a circle of healing. Indeed, the word "circle" itself is a metaphor for God's encompassing love that is revealed wherever two or three gather prayerfully.

In many communities of faith, persons kneel at the altar rail to receive Communion, healing touch, and anointing. At one healing service that we attend regularly, the healing team lays hands on the backs of those who kneel, channeling reiki healing touch, as the pastor anoints them. At the church where Kate is pastor, the person in search of healing for her- or himself, or for another for whom they are acting as a healing channel, comes to the center of the circle. As Kate lays her hands on the person's head, the others who are seeking healing also prayerfully reach out to touch the one in the center, in some cases giving reiki, along with their loving touch to the shoulders, back, arms, or hands. In both congregations, the community that remains seated is called to pray for those who seek healing. They do not need to know the details of the person for whom they pray. This act of spiritual solidarity reminds us that everyone in the community is in need of healing and that each person can be a channel of healing for others.

Praying and laying on of hands in any form is grace in action. It is a visible sign of God's universal grace that aims at blessing all things. Those of us who practice reiki, as a part of our healing ministry as Christians, make a commitment to become partners and co-creators in God's vision for healed persons and a healed planet. Some reiki practitioners, such as Bruce, use the sign of the cross along with the traditional reiki symbols, as a confession of our own loyalty to Jesus of Nazareth, and of our openness to the healing power that comes from his Spirit.

The profound intention to be a channel of divine energy was essential to the emergence of reiki in the United States. As a child, Hawayo Takata, who later brought reiki to America, prayed that God would give her the opportunity to use her hands for something other than manual labor. As she worked as a laborer in the sugar cane fields of a Hawaiian plantation, she pleaded, "God, please let me do better things with my hands and do not send me back to the cane field again, forever and ever."[3] God answered her prayer, and guided her journey to Japan and to an encounter with reiki healing touch. In the spirit of Hawayo Takata, many reiki practitioners begin their practice with a simple prayer, such as the one Bruce makes prior to each treatment and attunement.

> *Giver of life, love, and light,*
> *let your light shine through me.*
> *Let your healing light rest upon _____.*
> *Surround _____ with your love,*
> *grace, and protection,*

that he/she might experience the fullness of
your healing.
In Christ's name. Amen.

HEALING PRAYER

Physicians, scientists, and spiritual leaders are discovering that prayer is a non-local phenomenon. Our prayers radiate across the universe, creating a healing field of energy around and within those for whom we pray. Jesus' healing ministry involved direct touch and words of healing, but it also involved his mysterious power to heal at a distance. While the essence of prayer will always remain a mystery, we believe that our prayers weave themselves together with God's desire for the deepest good for all things in their unique context. Our own prayers may provide a "tipping point" that enables God's power to be more effective.

The practice of prayer involves centering ourselves in God, placing ourselves in the presence of God by aligning our deepest desires for healing and wholeness with God's deepest desires for healing and wholeness for the world. Prayer arises out of our silent wish to "be still and know that I am God" (Psalm 46:10). In the tumult of events, of hopes and disappointments, we can hear God's gentle voice of guidance, inspiration, and empowerment, if we but listen. As pioneers in Christian healing, Olga and Ambrose Worrall assert, "out of silence comes the power that heals."[4] Silence awakens our awareness of the "inner light," whose power, as the Quakers have long known, can energize our spirits and inspire us more fully to become God's agents of healing and justice.

Prayer also involves claiming the life-transforming power of being known in a loving way. The psalmist affirms the healing power of being known.

O Lord, you have searched me and known me. You know when I sit down and when I rise up; you discern my thoughts from far away. You search out my path and my lying down, and are acquainted with all my ways... Where can I go from your spirit? Or where can I flee from your presence? If I ascend to heaven, you are there; if I make my bed in Sheol you are there. If I take the wings of the morning and settle at the farthest limits of the sea, even there your hand shall lead me, and your right hand shall hold me fast. If I say, "Surely darkness shall cover me, and the light around me become night," even the darkness is not dark to you; the night is as bright as day, for darkness is as light to you.

Psalm 139:1–3, 7–13

In prayerful awareness, we recognize that wherever we are, we are in God's hands. Our Holy Companion will not abandon us, but gives us everything we need to find our way. In this encompassing acceptance, we discover that even our limitations and imperfections can become the media of healing.

In prayerful attentiveness, we awaken to the divine guidance that enables us to respond with healing and creativity to perplexing and problematic situations. In the words of the apostle Paul,

Likewise the Spirit helps us in our weakness; for we do not know how to pray as we ought, but that very Spirit intercedes with sighs too deep for words. And God, who searches the heart, knows

the mind of the Spirit, because the Spirit intercedes
for the saints according to the will of God.
Romans 8:26–27

God's voice sounds forth from the depths of our being in "sighs too deep for words." Attending to this creative sound of God, we experience the grace of knowing that God's voice inspires our prayers and that God weaves our prayers with the prayers of the universe to nurture healing in every situation. As Paul further notes, "in all things, God works for good" (Romans 8:28). Liberated from the need to guide or to control our own prayers, we simply let go and let God's wisdom and artistry creatively shape our prayers, as an artist shapes her or his colors on the canvas of life.

As prayer in action, reiki is both local and non-local. In the holistic ecology of life, there is no distinction between local and non-local. In touching another person, we bring wholeness to her or his body, mind, and spirit, and also create a field of healing energy that radiates beyond her or his particular psychophysical organism. In nurturing wholeness in one place, we bring wholeness to all places. In distant reiki, our focus on the well-being of another surrounds that person with God's healing light, gently altering her or his body, mind, spirit, and relationships.

As a form of intercessory prayer, reiki plays a role in transforming the past as well as the future. While we cannot change the fact that certain events have occurred, we can be partners in the "healing of memories" by transforming the meaning of a particular negative event.

Susan was the victim of physical and mental abuse in her first marriage. For years this abuse shaped her relationships and attitude toward life. In her 30s, Susan learned the first two levels of reiki and returned to a United Church of Canada congregation, where she committed herself to following Jesus through a life of prayer, meditation, and service.

Early in her journey as a Christian, Susan realized that forgiveness would be her greatest challenge. Though she accepted the healing Christ as her savior, she was still dominated by feelings of hatred, fear, and anger toward her first husband. While her reiki teacher and spiritual guide, along with her pastoral counselor, invited her to experience the totality of her feelings, they also challenged her to find God's healing touch in the midst of her pain. Her reiki teacher suggested that whenever she was overwhelmed by negative thoughts or emotions, Susan should take some time to center quietly, deeply feeling her emotions, and then invoke God's healing presence with the words "Nothing, not even this anger and fear, can separate me from the love of God." Following this, she asked Susan to begin giving herself a "distant" reiki treatment, by using her imagination to go back to her painful memories and to see them surrounded with the healing light of Christ and reiki healing touch. While the path to healing was not easy, Susan found herself on a new path. She has experienced a healing which has enabled her to let go of the domination of her past wounds, and to begin to trust others in loving relationships.

The practice of reiki as a prayer form can heal not only wounds of the past, but also worries for the future. When many of us ponder the future, we are trapped by fear and anxiety. Our blood pressure can soar and our anxiety spike as we anticipate an upcoming job interview, uncomfortable encounter, or unpleasant business or personal trip. In prayer, we imaginatively place this future event in God's hands, knowing that God will be our protection and strength in every circumstance. Through using reiki distant prayer, we can create a circle of grace and protection that can strengthen us and others for upcoming challenges.

Reiki healing prayer embraces past, present, and future. When a friend is having a job interview, traveling, or facing surgery, we imagine her surrounded by God's light and then give her a distant reiki treatment. As we imagine a future event in our own lives, we see this event encompassed by the light of God's universal energy, with the assurance that the God who has been our companion in the past will also accompany us in the future.

Today, scientific studies are confirming that prayer truly does change reality. While the operations of prayer can never be totally manipulated or fully understood, it is clear that we become God's partners in healing whenever we surround another person with prayer, healing imagery, healing light, or hands-on or distant reiki.

THE GIFTS OF SPIRITUAL FORMATION

The followers of the Way envisaged a community of caring in which persons would embody the mind of Christ in their daily lives. Christ was their deepest reality and greatest hope. God was not an external reality, distant from creation and humankind, but the inner voice of all creation and the animating principle of the human adventure.

Spiritual formation, whether group or individual, involves experiencing God's desire for shalom and wholeness for all creation. In connecting with God through the spiritual disciplines, we experience the energy of the vine that enables us to bear much fruit.

Today there is a growing interest in the spirituality of embodiment. As we reclaim the creation-affirming roots of our faith, we are learning to affirm that the heavens declare the glory of God and that our bodies reveal divine wisdom as well. Jesus' healing touch embraces every element of human life. To the woman who was healed from the burden of a gynecological disorder, Jesus affirmed, "Daughter, your faith has made you well; go in peace and be healed of your disease" (Mark 5:34). To the Samaritan leper who returned to give thanks to Jesus for his cure, Jesus proclaimed a healing of the spirit as well as the body: "Get up and go on your way; your faith has made you well" (Luke 17:19). Both people received a physical cure and a change in social status, but, more importantly, they received the gift of spiritual wholeness that would enable them to face every future trial and tribulation.

In holistic spiritual formation groups, we can promote healthy spiritual embodiment in a variety of ways: "body prayer," including physical movements that accompany chanting or spoken prayers; liturgical dance, in which moving with God's spirit embraces our whole being; simple yoga exercises to enhance spiritual centering and vital energy; simple meditative breath prayers, which focus the mind and embrace the enveloping Spirit; and healing touch, through rituals of laying on of hands, the use of various healing arts such as reiki, and anointing. Walking prayer, characteristic of the Benedictine tradition, is yet another holistic devotional resource, which integrates biblical reflection, quiet centering, and intentional movement.

Reiki is a form of body prayer that enables us to see our bodies as reflections of divine love, worthy of love and affirmation. As we allow the energy of love to flow through us, we affirm our place as members of Christ's healing body.

The practice of reiki enables us to avoid the subtle and not-so-subtle forms of body-denial and hatred that have infected

Christianity from the first century. Though those forms of Gnosticism that scorned the body and physical existence were labeled a heresy by the early church, 20 centuries of Christian spirituality have continued to see the body as an impediment to spiritual growth. Reiki reveals the beauty and wisdom of our bodies, and the connection of our whole being with God's creative love. Reiki affirms the wisdom of the incarnation – "the Word became flesh and lived among us, and we have seen his glory, the glory of God's only son, full of grace and truth" (John 1:14). In inspiring us to love our bodies gracefully, reiki grounds traditional spiritual formation practices and enables us to affirm God's presence in the holy embodiment of nature and the non-human world.

THE HEALING CHURCH

We believe that in its many voices, scripture gives a lively and powerful word to people today. Unbound from the chains of fundamentalism and enlightened by the discoveries of the new physics and the healing arts such as reiki, the scriptures address each one of us with words of hope, challenge, acceptance, transformation, and empowerment as never before. By imaginatively approaching the scriptures through contemporary forms of traditional spiritual practices – such as *lectio divina*, the multi-sensory approach of the Ignatian spiritual exercises, and the use of guided meditations – we can experience God at work in our lives with the same care and inspiration that characterized God's presence in biblical times.[5] God's voice sounds through our hearts and divine energy flows through our hands with the same power that declared itself 2000 years ago in the life of Jesus the Healer. Jesus is speaking to us today just as he did to his own ambivalent and imperfect disciples.

*Proclaim the good news, "The kingdom of heaven
has come near." Cure the sick, raise the dead,
cleanse the lepers, cast out demons...*
Matthew 10:7–8

Can you be an intentional member of the body of Christ, able to fulfill your role as a healer or a miracle worker just as easily as other roles you might assume, such as teacher, nurse, and administrator? Is God saying to your church, "You are to be a light to the nations"? and, to you individually, "You are the light of the world"? The answer is "yes!"

In all its many roles, the church is called to be a temple of healing and wholeness. In addition to our own unique gifts, each one of us is called to be a healer – one who seeks to be an instrument of God's grace and wholeness. In this spirit, many churches have initiated congregational health ministry or parish nursing programs. Inspired by Christ's compassion and the vision of shalom that unites spirituality and health, persons and communities, a growing number of churches are initiating healing services along with programs for congregational and community health. Certain churches, such as the Palisades Community Church, in Washington, D.C., have placed reiki at the heart of their healing ministry.[6]

Whether led by parish nurses, laypersons, or clergy, congregational health ministries seek to join spiritual, physical, and communal well-being, thus providing an alternative to Western medicine's emphasis on the body as the primary focus of health. Congregational health ministries share the healing light of Christ through as diverse but simple means as medical interventions, preventive health care, education, and pastoral care. They provide companionship for shut-ins and support for caregivers at home. They also position themselves to be "squeaky wheels" in their advocacy for persons in hospitals and nursing homes.

Often congregational health care givers fill out forms and review the various bureaucratic hoops and barriers with people, in order to help them access benefits available to them through medicare and various insurance plans. Congregational health care givers recognize that hospitals and nursing homes are stretched to the breaking point. Cost cutting has made it impossible for patients to receive the level of care that will facilitate their optimal recovery. Further, well-intended social workers and government employees are often hemmed in by massive client loads and burdensome regulations. Congregational health care givers can be the voice of compassion as well as of assertiveness in difficult medical situations. To paraphrase an African proverb, "it takes a village to insure the health of a child or adult." The church is, for many, the village where personal healing and wholeness at every stage of life is given top priority.

Some congregational health ministries join prevention, advocacy, education, and health screening with services of healing, involving laying on of hands or anointing with oil. In all these situations, pastors and laypersons seek to embody the spirit of Teresa of Avila, who affirmed that

> You are Christ's hands.
> Christ has no body now on earth but yours,
> no hands but yours, no feet but yours.
> Yours are the eyes through which Christ's compassion is to look upon the world.
> Yours are the feet with which [God] is to go about doing good.
> Yours are the hands through which [God] is to bless women and men now.[7]

Reiki healing touch provides a dimension of palliative care that is absent from many congregational health programs. Grounded in respect for privacy and bodily autonomy, reiki healing touch can provide relief from chronic pain; reduce stress among caregivers who spend much of the day taking care of a homebound spouse, parent, or child; support the emotional healing of the bereaved; and boost the immune system and provide hope among persons who are diagnosed with terminal illnesses.

Sickness often constricts our reality. To the patient or her or his family, the world may shrink to the size of their hospital room, apartment, or home. By contrast, touch connects and expands our vision of reality. Healing touch radiates through body, mind, and spirit, restoring our hope, relieving our anxiety, and reminding us that we are never alone.

Jesus sent his disciples out "two by two" to teach, preach, and heal. Perhaps Jesus recognized that such intentional partnerships give us confidence and courage in difficult situations, as well as call us to accountability. Where "two or three are gathered in Christ's name," healing power is released. Friends of the Spirit invite the Healer to create what Celtic spirituality calls a "thin place," an environment where eternity breaks through the everyday. Similarly, a reiki healing ministry is most effectively carried out by pairs of practitioners, whose healing spirits and hands support each other and bring a spirit of empowerment to the persons to whom they minister.

Within the community of faith, a reiki healing ministry is most helpful when it is placed in the context of the church's wider congregational health and healing ministry. As we discussed in the previous chapter, instruction in the practice of Christian reiki is given in the context of studying the healings of Jesus; the current interplay of spirituality and health; the importance of ethical principles, confidentiality, boundaries, and healthy touch; as well as the reiki positions, attunements, and the relationship between reiki and other holistic and complementary medical approaches. If reiki is to find a spiritual home in a church's health and healing ministry, the initiation of a reiki healing ministry must be grounded in careful discernment of the congregation's unique gifts and challenges, education on the nature of reiki and its relationship to Christian faith, and exploration of other healing modalities, such as anointing, intercessory prayer, and the laying on of hands. Just as the initiation of a healing ministry and the rituals of healing require a sound approach to Christian theology and a clear response to stereotypes and negative attitudes, the initiation of a reiki healing ministry in the church requires that leaders respond to concerns among more traditional members that reiki's connection with Buddhism and use by New Age healers will compromise the purity of the gospel message.

While we cannot allay everyone's concerns regarding the orthodoxy of healing ministries in general, and reiki healing in particular, we can clearly affirm that Jesus used the energy and power of God to heal, and that this power may be similar in kind to the chi of Chinese medicine and the prana of Ayurvedic medicine. We must continually return to the wisdom of the early Christian theologians who asserted that "wherever truth is present, God is its source." If reiki brings relief, healing, or comfort, then we can boldly affirm that reiki is an instrument of God.

Today, many persons are in search of healing and wholeness. They recognize that spirituality and health are profoundly interconnected. A church that provides opportunities for spiritual growth, healing services, theological reflection, and hands-on healing will be a mecca for seekers and persons interested in a deeper relationship with God. The church will come alive as the energy of love bursts forth in hospital rooms, pastoral care encounters, and lively worship and healing services. With Hildegard of Bingen, we can affirm that such a church will be flexible, growing, and green in spirit, and its light will bring healing to persons and communities.

> *Good people,*
> *most royal greening verdancy,*
> *rooted in the sun,*
> *you shine with radiant light.*
> *In this circle of earthly existence,*
> *you shine so finely,*
> *it surpasses understanding.*
> *God hugs you.*
> *You are encircled*
> *by the arms*
> *of the mystery of God.*[8]

With reiki healing touch, God touches us and heals us, and enables us to touch and hug others into wholeness and connection at every point in life's journey

MENDING THE WORLD

Recently, at a spiritual growth group that Bruce facilitated, one of the members asked, "Didn't Jesus' ministry focus on the spiritual and not the physical?" Because her viewpoint represented what many Christians presume to be orthodox theology, the questioner was surprised when Bruce replied, "Yes, but." Yes, Jesus was deeply concerned with our spiritual lives, with our eternal destiny as children of God and as participants in God's heavenly reign. But Jesus also recognized that the spiritual and the physical dimensions of life can't be separated. Jesus preached to the crowds, but he also fed them. Jesus called people to repentance and to spiritual transformation, but he also healed their bodies. Jesus focused on the needs of the individual in front of him, but his inclusion of women, tax collectors, outcasts, foreigners, and persons with chronic illnesses and disabilities challenged the established social order among his own people, the Jews, as well as the Roman oppressors. Jesus' vision of reality joined body and spirit, secular and sacred, individual and social. Jesus' vision of shalom includes all things, including economics and politics.

In contrast to Jesus' holistic approach to wholeness and healing, Gary Gunderson notes that,

> [M]ost of the work linking spirituality and health reflects our individualistic perspective. We want to harness spirituality like another vitamin or diet scheme for our personal gain. Or we might employ it as a therapeutic strategy for individual patients. This works on a limited basis, of course, but it misses the point. The great power comes from a sense of finding one's place in the universe and finding that that place is a gift of a gracious God.[9]

Jesus' ministry affirmed that health is ultimately relational and communal in nature. In its embodiment of shalom – God's reign of harmony, justice, and peace – health includes the totality of our lives and not just our bodies or eternal destiny. We cannot be fully healthy as individuals apart from healthy relationships; a clean and life-supporting personal, social, and natural environment; and the embodiment of mercy and justice in our institutional and political lives. In the words of the Christian Medical Commission of the World Council of Churches,

> *Health and wholeness is a dynamic state of well-being of the individual and the society; of spiritual, mental, economic, political, and social well-being; of being in harmony with each other, the natural environment, and with God.*[10]

While we must encourage the practices of prayer, meditation, and healing touch, we also must remember that our health and the health of others is profoundly social in nature. As Gary Gunderson notes, studies indicate that "the most reliable predictor of a person's long-term health is not access to medical services, but one's educational level, which is best understood as a function of the economic status of one's parents."[11]

The Jewish tradition often speaks of the ultimate goal of personal spiritual formation as *tikkun olam*, "mending the world." We heal the planet and our communities through our prayers and healing touch, but also by our commitment to acts of mercy and justice.[12]

Early in his healing ministry, Mikao Usui recognized the social implications of reiki healing. Following his mystical revelation of reiki touch healing, Usui decided to go to the slums of Kyoto, where he would give treatments and invite the beggars who lived there to go to a nearby monastery where they would be trained in employable skills. In order to insure his safety, Usui sought out the protection of the chief of the beggars. His only requirements were that he be given a place to sleep and teach reiki, along with three bowls of rice each day. Usui gave reiki treatments in the slums for several years. But he became discouraged when he realized that many of the persons he healed and sent into the community returned to the slums. Many had found that working for a living was much more difficult than they had imagined. In order to move ahead, they needed more than just job training and physical healing, they needed spiritual formation and character development. According to the reiki story, his recognition of the need to integrate spiritual and physical well-being inspired Usui to utilize the following ethical principles in the teaching of reiki:

> *Just for today, do not worry.*
> *Just for today, do not be angry.*
> *Honor your teachers, your parents,*
> *your neighbors, your friends.*
> *Give thanks for all living things.*
> *Earn your living honestly.*[13]

Today, our practice of Christian reiki must go beyond individual well-being. The practice of reiki, like Jesus' healing ministry, joins the personal and social dimensions of life. As we heal one another, we are contributing to the healing of the community. But more than that, we can utilize the practice of reiki to transform families, relationships, meetings, and institutions.

In his book *Claiming All Things for God*, United Methodist social leader George McLain calls us to be contemplative-activists. McLain believes that the church is called to be a participant in the healing and cleansing of institutions through joining prayer, spiritual formation, and social action. As an embodiment of God's healing light, followers of Christ's way are challenged to be a "light to the nations." Weaving together reiki healing touch and prayer can bring transformation to our church meetings and institutional structures.

Virtually all of us recognize that certain physical spaces can be healing or toxic to mind, body, spirit, and relationships. In a similar fashion, imperfect social and political institutions promote well-being, as well as injustice and pain. As Walter Wink notes, in describing the spirit that can dominate a group or institution,

> *The powers are good.*
> *The powers are fallen.*
> *The powers can be redeemed.*[14]

Yet institutional healing must first begin at home, within the family and the local congregation. Reiki promotes healing at home when we regularly give reiki treatments to our spouses, children, and other relatives, and when we surround our home with reiki healing power. In filling our homes with divine energy, we claim our homes as places of love, growth, and healing – as sanctuaries that send us forth into the world with compassion and commitment.

In the Celtic spiritual tradition, there are many prayers of "encompassing" or "encircling." In these prayers, one invokes the awareness of God while drawing a circle around oneself or one's environment with the index finger. In a similar context, reiki can be employed in the healing, cleansing, and affirmation of a home. As you awaken to God's healing light in your household, simply make the reiki symbols or join them with the sign of the cross as you enter each room and as you walk around your home either physically or imaginatively. As it is prepared, the family's food can be infused with reiki healing power. Reiki, along with other spiritual disciplines, cleanses negative thinking, angry words, and pain with the divine beauty and love that flows through all things.

McLain speaks of cleansing a church meeting in a similar fashion. In describing a particular church meeting, McLain notes that prior to the meeting, each person at the meeting was assigned to pray for a part of the room, asking for the healing and cleansing of all negative powers and principalities. Together, they spoke words of transformation and healing as a way to claim the space for God.

> *Remove from this space any spirit of worldly ambition and competition. Remove from this space the powers of closed-mindedness, that keep the faithful from hearing one another. Remove from this space the power of fear that keeps faithful Christians from daring to be brave and true to the gospel of love as given to us by Jesus Christ. Remove from this space all the powers and principalities that prevent the gathered church from being the true body of Christ, in ministry to one another and all the world, in the spirit of justice, righteousness, and love.*[15]

While McLain's practice of spiritual cleansing of a room is as foreign to some Christians as reiki healing, the joining of reiki to social, spatial, and spiritual cleansing empowers our participation in God's all-encompassing healing work. Reiki practitioners can encircle the room and the meeting itself with reiki healing touch. During the time of the meeting, one person could be given the responsibility for prayerful attentiveness to the meeting as he or she surrounds it with the spirit of divine love and communion through distant reiki.

McLain suggests that we pray for the cleansing of institutions, corporate meetings, and places where injustice has occurred in the following manner:

1. Focus on the details of the institutional meeting.
2. Include yourself among those for whom you pray.
3. Pray for the cleansing of any ungodly spirit.
4. Pray that Christ fill everyone who is present.
5. Move around the room or building, praying for that space and meeting physically by your presence or in your imagination.
6. Thank God for divine healing of the powers and principalities and the institution involved.
7. Continue in intercession during the course of the event.

Like McLain's spiritual cleansing process, reiki calls us to choose always to be on the side of spiritual hope and transformation, to use our hands for healing and not violence, and to clothe our behaviors in the garments of mercy, justice, and reconciliation. We can utilize present or non-local reiki in every social encounter. Our concern for healing touch inspires us to care for the well-being of the persons we may never meet. Though intensely personal and hands-on in nature, we affirm that our healing touch calls us to become agents of healing and reconciliation in our society by promoting the cause of adequate health care for all persons, by embodying love and justice in our care for the environment and for our non-human companions, and by reaching out to the vulnerable and neglected.

For many of us, this also means advocating for political and economic policies that fairly distribute medical supplies and food aid, as well as working for structures of justice that support self-determination among the impoverished in our land and across the world. In the spirit of "the butterfly effect," apparently insignificant actions performed on a consistent basis can change the world. Meeting by meeting, treatment by treatment, touch by touch, we mend the world as we surround all things with the healing light of Christ. Radiating across our homes, our churches, our nation and its institutions, and across the planet, our gentle reiki touch, when joined to our actions and the prayers of others, creates a field of force that makes room for the incarnation of healing and love in all things.

RITUALS THAT HEAL[16]

Worship orients persons toward the source of all healing and wholeness. In worship, we affirm that God's healing love not only surrounds us, but arises from the depths of our being and bursts forth in the actions of healing touch, symbols, and songs. In worship, we recognize that God's love is the source of the original wholeness that grounds creation's journey and that inspires our own healing adventures. In remembering that we live, move, and have our being in God's creative and transformative energy of love, we are inspired to let that love flow through us by our words, touch, silence, presence, forgiveness, or intercession. Out of the abundance of God's love, we mediate God's healing touch to our neighbor.

The service that follows is grounded in the dual recognition that healing comes through a variety of media and that each person uniquely reflects God's healing love. We are, as Martin Luther asserts, "little Christs," who are called to share with our neighbor the salvation and wholeness we have ourselves received. In sharing God's wholeness with others, we experience God's healing working within our own lives. In God's circle of healing, we are called to heal others.

While this service was initially written to celebrate the initiation of 30 Christian reiki healers at the Kirkridge Conference Center, it can be adapted to any healing context. We invite you to shape this service for your own community's needs and mission. There is no one approach to worship, healing, or wholeness. Regardless of cultural, liturgical, and theological expression, wherever healing occurs, God is its source and inspiration.

A Service of Healing & Blessing

Touched by God

THE CALL TO AWARENESS
Touched by Water

Silent Opening to the Wholeness of God –
Remembering Our Original Wholeness
Remembrance of Our First Touch

One: It is most unfortunate that none of us can consciously
remember our first moment...
that time, when, through the touch of God's love,
we each individually came to be.
How instantaneous that moment...like water...running
between our fingers...
fluid, fleeting, hard to grasp, impossible to articulate,
but in our own unique moment of creation,

we each personally experienced God's first touch...
replete with original wholeness and love,
and repeatedly echoed by all other touch
found in nurture and care throughout our lives.
And so, we bathe our hands this morning...
not because we must – but because we may...
not because we need to in any way, but because we want to,
because we want to remember something beyond words,
back in a moment before we even had words,
back to our very first gift, the first touch of God...

Words of Prayer upon the Water

All: **In the openness of our outstretched hands, there is always vulnerability.**
     In our responsive care extended to others, there is always acceptance.
     In the gentle strength of your healing touch,
     you will always reveal your love.

The Sacrament of Healing Touch: Consecrating Our Hands to God's Healing

Basin and towel are carried from participant to participant.
Each person's hands are carefully bathed, and then dried.

THE CALL TO OPENNESS
Touched by God's Word

The Scripture
     John 10:10

Silent Reflection

Shared Reflection

> *Blessing our silence and words (giving thanks for the insights we have found individually and as a group).*

THE CALL TO GRACE
Touched by God through the
Laying on of Hands & Anointing with Oil

The Scriptures

> Psalm 133
>
> Matthew 6:25–34

Prayer over the Oil

> Anointing with oil
>
> The laying on of hands

Prayers of the People: Petitions and Intercessions

THE CALL TO LOVE ONE ANOTHER
Touched by Communion

Invitation: Vine and branches (John 15:1, 4–7)

Eucharistic Prayer

Pastor: God be with you.

People: And also with you.

Pastor: Let us open our hearts to God.

People: In wonder and awe, we claim God's love and are made whole.

Pastor: Let us give thanks to God.

People: For Holy Love is infinite and everlasting.

Pastor: We give you thanks, O God of infinite love and creativity, for your constant presence in all things.

> You are the heart of all creation, and in holy love

we joyfully live, move, and have our being.
Your beauty and wisdom bring forth universe after
universe:
both those worlds within us, and the multitude of
worlds infinitely beyond ourselves.
Your artistry brings forth the earth and colors
all living things.
All creation breathes your spirit. All creatures embody
your love.
Your holy adventure is heard in the cries of babes.
It inspires the voices of prophets. It whispers in
the mundane words of women and men of
every tradition and place.
In original wholeness, your beauty is constantly revealed
as our deepest identity.
As your beloved children, our most basic essence is
holy love.
We give you thanks, for the wisdom incarnate in
Jesus of Nazareth,
the healer and lover, our faithful friend for the heart's
journey to you.
In Christ, we celebrate your gift of open vision and
gentle power
that reclaims the wholeness that is your intention for
all things.
In Christ, all wounds are healed, all sin forgiven,
all alienation reconciled.
In Christ, all suffering is cherished and transformed.
Let your Spirit, O Loving Companion, break forth in
our voice, as we and all creation
give voice to the sighs too deep for words:

All: **Holy, holy, holy Love.**

Everything resonates with your touch.

With joy, we embrace your care that creates and responds.

All things proclaim your love.

We join with you to celebrate healing and goodness.

In Christ, your tender strength is revealed.

You have brought love to life, and life to love.

Pastor: We remember your infinite love for all creation, revealed in Christ's love for us.

In the midst of suffering, love is victorious.

In the midst of death, new life springs forth.

In Christ's suffering and death, in the body and blood, the bread and wine, our suffering is transformed and our wounds are healed.

In sharing Christ's bread and wine, all meals and all touch are made holy.

As our bodies and relationships are made whole, your loving promise is fulfilled.

All: **Let your Spirit transform our lives as we share in the bread and the wine. May the bread and wine reveal to us your healing love so that we might become co-creators in your holy adventure. Enable your love to heal in word and touch, in silence and in prayer.**

Pastor: These are the gifts of God, given to God's people. Our sharing in them unites us and all others with God in the adventure of healing and wholeness.

Sharing the Bread and the Cup

THE CALL TO PARTNERSHIP
Touched by Presence

The Invitation

One: God is the circle whose center is everywhere and whose circumference is nowhere. We are always in the divine circle; we are always home; we are always loved, and our light and love radiates across the Universe.

Forming the Healing Circle

One: As a sign of the healing circle that encompasses all things, let us be a circle of love and healing, let us open ourselves to the flow of God's healing light, sharing healing with one another through the touch of hands and tender words of prayer.

(A time of embracing in light, love, and peace.)

Sending Forth in the Circle of Love

One: Let us go forth always in the circle of love. Go in peace. Go in light. Go in health. Amen.

5

REIKI IN PASTORAL CARE

*You are the light of the world... let your light
shine before others, so that they may see your
good works and give glory to your [Parent] in
heaven.*

Matthew 5:14, 16

You shine like stars in the world.

Philippians 2:15

*I was sick and you took care of me... as you did
it to one of the least of these who are members of
my family, you did it to me.*

Matthew 25:36, 40

As followers of the way of Jesus and reiki healing touch, our aim is to bring healing to every encounter. The whole community of faith is called to claim its role as "the light of the world," letting God's light flow through its worship and service to bring wholeness, salvation, and reconciliation to the world. In the spirit of the Protestant affirmation of "the priesthood of all believers," the practice of reiki provides a way in which all persons – even those who do not consider themselves to be healers – can participate in the healing touch of God.

The mission of the church is to be a community of caring and healing, especially toward the vulnerable and weak. In the body of Christ, the love we give to others ripples across the universe and eventually back to ourselves. In the ecology of life, each one of us will eventually become one, or more, of "the least of these" – the bereaved, the dying, the chronically ill, the disabled, or the economically insecure. At such times, we will need words of love and acts of mercy. We will need to accept the grace that we have shared with others. In this chapter, we explore the importance of reiki healing touch in the pastoral ministry of the church as it relates to three of life's crises – hospitalization, chronic disease, and terminal illness. In each of these conditions of life, reiki mediates God's healing touch to bring comfort, peace, and wholeness.

At The Palisades Community Church in Washington, D.C., under Kate's pastoral leadership and Bruce's teaching ministry, the practice of reiki became an essential part of the church's healing and congregational health care ministry. Bruce taught several members of the church how to use reiki for self-care and outreach to others. During Kate's ten years as pastor, hospitalized members have come to expect, and often request, reiki and other forms of healing touch from their pastor and fellow parishioners. Woven through virtually every aspect of the ministry of this ecumenical church, reiki has become an integral part of its spiritual formation and mission.

In the following pages, we will describe how reiki has made a difference in the pastoral ministry of this 175-member congregation. It is also important to note that

The Palisades Community Church is in many ways an "average" Christian congregation. Its parishioners seldom seek or expect miraculous deliverance from illness or life's challenges. They do not anticipate immunity from life's trials or supernatural intervention to solve their problems. But they have come to recognize the importance of a spiritual path that embraces prayer, meditation, laying on of hands, worship, and service. Reiki healing touch has become a central aspect of their worship and spiritual formation.

REIKI AT THE HOSPITAL

People often feel most alone and vulnerable in the hospital setting. Every medical diagnosis and intervention reminds us of our mortality. The hospital's "stripping process" in which patients must give up their clothing, medications, and privacy typically disempowers even the most assertive persons. Though comfort and curing are the goals of medical profession and the hospital, patients typically feel frightened, anxious, and manipulated by the institutional culture of Western medicine. Surrounded by the hustle and bustle of nurses, technicians, aides, and physicians, patients often feel alone and disconnected from the healing resources of the universe.

In the hospital setting, reiki healing touch provides comfort, reassurance, and connection. Reiki enhances the patient's sense of empowerment by connecting her or him to a larger healing reality and by reminding them that they can be partners in their own healing process. Further, reiki may reduce the negative side effects of medical interventions, as well as promote the overall healing process. Reiki complements and supports whatever medical procedures are being employed for the patient's well-being not only by balancing and enhancing the divine healing energy, but also by visibly witnessing to God's presence in times of crisis and need.

I (Kate) have found reiki to be a helpful adjunct to traditional pastoral care in the hospital setting. Reiki is not only palliative, but remarkable in its effects when persons are hospitalized. In both pre-operative and emergency room settings, I most often lay one or both of my hands on the top of the patient's head when I pray for her or him. As I pray verbally for the healing of mind, body, and spirit, I wordlessly support the patient's mental and spiritual harmony by invoking the appropriate reiki symbols. Even persons who have not experienced reiki healing touch prior to their hospitalization inevitably close their eyes, relax, and deepen their breathing. Amid the storm of medical preparations, they feel a sense of calm centeredness.

If I am waiting with someone scheduled for surgery, who has become impatient and anxious as a result of scheduling delays or procedural confusion, I have found that simply leaving my hand on their brow or forehead almost always eases their anxiety and promotes serenity. One person who responded to a surgical delay with a bout of hiccoughs was amazed to have them disappear after a brief reiki treatment.

When our son Matt was scheduled to have surgery for an angiofibroma, a rare form of vascular tumor near the brain, Bruce and I delayed the surgery for a month, after consulting with the surgeon, in order to give Matt reiki treatments several times a day. He also received a weekly healing treatment from a Christian woman, known for her gift of healing touch. We hoped that the tumor would completely disappear. Prior to the surgery, the radiologist conjectured that the reiki may have made a difference, noting that the MRI indicated that "the tumor didn't go away, but it didn't grow either. I think you should lay hands on his surgeon, too!" We not only laid hands on his surgeon prior to the surgery, but sent our son and the surgical team distant reiki throughout the nine-and-one-half-hour surgery. Needless to say, a circle of friends surrounded our family with prayer and reiki throughout the long ordeal. Their presence helped ease our own sense of anxiety and powerlessness during those interminable hours.

Following surgery, nurses checking their patients' vital signs have often marveled at the quick return to normal body temperature and respiration. Happily, in recent years, when nurses have noted the change and asked me what I have done to facilitate the transformation, they acknowledge the power of reiki and its effects and usually thank me for my support. Many of them quietly and anonymously practice reiki or other forms of healing touch as they move from patient to patient. Their use of reiki witnesses to the partnership between medicine and spirituality that is often hidden in the hospital setting.

In the aftermath of a radical mastectomy, one parishioner experienced an irregular heartbeat (tachycardia). She claims that her heartbeat returned to normal the minute I laid hands on her. At the time, I was not even aware of her predicament. My primary intent was simply to address the surgical wound by giving a reiki treatment a few inches over the surface of her skin. But because I believed I was assisting the healing process in its entirety, I was also indirectly promoting her mental and cardiovascular well-being. Focused or not, reiki, like prayer, responds to whatever personal needs are most pressing.

Several of Bruce's reiki students have reported their physicians' amazement when broken bones knitted together in half the expected time due to their daily self-reiki treatments on the affected area. Regular post-surgical reiki treatments have played a role in relieving abdominal gas pains following surgery and in the re-establishment of bowel functioning following bowel resection.

I always ask for permission from the medical staff before giving reiki to anyone in intensive care. In order not to disrupt the various monitors, I usually administer reiki only at the head and feet of the patient. In my experience, even when persons are unconscious, they are able to recall my presence and the laying on of hands, although they cannot remember my exact words. Reiki healing touch responds to both our conscious and unconscious need for healing and connection at those times when we are most vulnerable.

REIKI, CANCER, AND CHRONIC ILLNESS

I (Bruce) regularly work with persons with cancer and other chronic illnesses. Often I meet with them following their chemotherapy treatments. Our sessions weave together spiritual direction, meditation, and reiki healing touch.

After briefly checking in, we spend ten to 20 minutes doing an imaginative meditation on God's healing light. In this meditation, one simply breathes in divine light, letting it fill one's body, mind, and spirit from head to toe, with particular focus on the primary cancer site. This imaginative meditation is also helpful during chemotherapy and radiation treatments. I often counsel people receiving chemotherapy treatments to visualize the light infusing their body along with the chemotherapy, or permeating their body along with the radiation. This approach enables them to see their treatments as a spiritual discipline, as a sacrament of divine healing, rather than as a "necessary evil" whose side effects are often perceived as worse than the disease. It also enables them to remain calm, spiritually centered, and personally empowered amid the hustle and bustle of the medical environment.

Virtually everyone to whom I have provided this combination of reiki and spiritual formation has reported only modest side effects from their medical treatments. As a result of spiritually reframing their experience, some have accepted chemotherapy and radiation as divine gifts to be embraced rather than merely tolerated.

During the period of spiritual conversation, we reflect prayerfully on the divine presence within the cancer experience. While I avoid the typical evangelical Christian and New Age platitudes that often surround the diagnosis of cancer – such as cancer is "a lesson to be learned," "a spiritual test," "divine punishment," "the result of one's thinking," or "a divine gift" – my intention is to enable persons to experience God as a benevolent force working for growth, healing, and stature within every aspect of their lives, including their experience of cancer.

While there is no guarantee that their spiritual commitments will lead to a cure of the disease, the interplay of reiki and spiritual discipline almost always leads to healing of the whole person, that is, a sense of peaceful confidence that God is with them and that whatever the outcome of the disease, their lives will be in God's hands.

We conclude our time with a reiki treatment and a closing prayer. Often, when I give a reiki treatment following chemotherapy or radiation treatments, the recipient falls asleep or enters a sleep-like state. At such times, reiki provides both palliation and the gentle assurance that the person is in God's faithful care.

I have also found reiki to palliate, or lessen, the symptoms associated with chronic ailments such as arthritis, migraine headaches, and ALS.

Susan suffered from chronic migraine headaches. Sometimes the pain was so debilitating that she was forced to take off work or cancel recreational activities with her family. When she came to see me, Susan was desperate. She had tried virtually every Western medical approach and still saw herself as a victim of the migraines that had tormented her for years.

While I encouraged her to continue seeing her Western physician, I also suggested that Susan embark upon a spiritual, emotional, and physical adventure that included daily centering prayer; visualization exercises involving imaging divine light healing and soothing her pain; regular reiki treatments and self-reiki; and acupuncture treatments with a well-respected practitioner.

Today Susan is virtually migraine-free. When she feels the symptoms of a migraine coming on, she immediately lies down and begins to visualize God's healing light permeating her body and flowing through her blood vessels while she gives herself a reiki treatment. Typically, this time of personal centering and self-care either reduces or alleviates her pain completely.

Susan's condition has also benefited from her husband's personal support. Inspired by his wife's quest for wholeness, Steve learned reiki and regularly gives Susan reiki treatments. Susan jokes that they have become a "reiki family." Steve and Susan not only give one another regular reiki treatments, but also bathe their children in reiki healing touch. They report that their children have had fewer colds and sinus infections since they began to give them reiki treatments. Although their children are currently too young to learn traditional reiki, Steve and Susan also note that their children lay their hands on their parents as a sign of love and support when the adults seem fatigued or depressed.

At the heart of my approach to reiki training is self-reiki for prevention, well-being, and palliation, or lessening or easing of symptoms. Accordingly, virtually everyone who comes to me in order to receive a reiki treatment eventually learns level one reiki for their own well-being. After they learn the first level of reiki, they now have a ready-to-hand tool they can use to respond creatively to their illness.

The integration of reiki and spiritual practices with Western and complementary medical techniques is a source of personal empowerment and centeredness for persons dealing with chronic illnesses of mind, body, and spirit.

DEATH AND BEREAVEMENT

The dying process is a "thin place," where time and eternity meet. At the edges of life, we are often more open to God's desire for healing and wholeness. We realize that we are entering life's final journey and need to make peace with God, our family and our closest friends, and our own personal histories. As "near-death experiences" suggest, we can experience God's forgiveness and companionship even at the moment of death and, we suspect, beyond the grave. But for most of us, in times of crisis, God is most fully incarnate in the loving hands and healing words of trusted friends and family members who serve as companions for this final earthly adventure. We need to feel God's touch mediated through the loving hands of our companions.

I (Kate) have had the privilege of administering reiki in several hospice settings, and have coached persons in centering prayer and other techniques for opening to God's presence during the transition from life to death. In each case, the persons involved were diagnosed with late stage cancer and wanted to be as creative as possible before the progress of their illness and the morphine, prescribed for palliative reasons, could deprive them of clear consciousness. They seemed to appreciate reiki as a form of both "comfort care" to relieve pain, and as an inspiration and support for their focused spiritual reflection and centering.

A recent experience I had reveals the power of reiki to comfort and transform. On a quiet New Year's morning at a Bethesda, Maryland, nursing facility, I was present with Emily as she made the transition from nearly two years of suffering with cancer to a peaceful death in the arms of God. For two hours prior to her death, I sat with her, comforting her with words of scripture (Psalm 23 and Psalm 121), gentle supportive conversation, and reiki healing touch. As Emily's breathing became more labored, I assured her that God was with her and then invited her to experience "God's light." In that moment, Emily breathed her last breath and took the first steps on her next spiritual adventure.

Throughout her dying process, I visited Emily regularly, bringing her the comfort of scripture, news from the church, assurance that her financial affairs were in order, and reiki healing touch. She had come to expect that when we prayed together, we would take a generous amount of time for silence, in which she centered on the divine as I laid hands on her head and feet.

As Christians, we believe that death is not the end of our journey with Christ. While the exact process of transition will always be a mystery for the living, the image of a "long tunnel," described by those who have had near-death experiences, reflects the possibility that there may be a time of transition between this life and the next stage of our holy adventure with God.

It is our experience that a person's spirit may linger for some hours after death. On one occasion, after spending several hours at the hospital with family members following the death of Agnes, from complications related to Alzheimer's disease, the family asked me to say a final prayer of passage. Although one of the sons was still on his way to the hospital, we gathered in a circle holding hands and opening ourselves to this holy moment. As the husband of 60 years took his wife's hand, I felt drawn to complete the circle by placing my hand upon her forehead. To my amazement, as we prayed, I sensed a great heat emanating from her forehead, despite the fact that the body, by this time, was quite cold. It was clear to me that Agnes' spirit was waiting for her son to join us in the circle of love. Synchronously, her son arrived shortly thereafter and was able to join the family circle before Agnes' physical body was taken to the morgue.

Certain mystical streams of both Judaism and Christianity affirm the post-mortem journey of the soul. In the mystical Judaism of the Kabbalah, the soul's initial post-mortem journey is described in terms of a process of confession, acceptance, and purification. During this time, our prayers and thoughts can ease the transition from this world to the next. While Protestants typically see the transition from this life to God's heavenly realm as immediate and abrupt, the Catholic imagery of purgatory and the practice of prayers for the dead remind us that in the ecology of God's care, the living and the dead are joined. In this time of spiritual transition, our prayers and reiki treatments for the deceased not only provide a sense of comfort and connection for those who are living, but may also enable the deceased to let go of this life more gently in order to embrace the possibilities of new life in companionship with God.

As Christians, we must affirm that God is the companion of both the living and the dead. The love that brought us into life and that guided us in our earthly adventure receives us in death and inspires us in the next steps of our spiritual journey. As we breathe our last breath, our own breath is joined with the divine breath that revives us for the adventures ahead. Grace abounds in this life and the next.

The use of reiki as an essential part of my pastoral ministry does not end at the funeral and graveside services. Those who grieve face significant challenges in letting go of the deceased and embracing new possibilities for growth and transformation. Medical research notes that during the first year following the death of a spouse or a child, the rate of mortality and physical and mental illness radically increases. Further, the stresses of not only caring for a dying child, but also living together as a couple following her or his death are often too great for many marriages to bear. When parishioners are going through the grief process, I regularly join my prayers with distant reiki in order to enhance God's healing presence in their lives. As with all prayer, we do not pre-ordain the results, but join God in creating a spiritual environment in which health and wholeness may gently emerge from life's most painful situations.

I endured repeated losses when I was a child and I have struggled with unresolved grief from these experiences throughout my life. Bruce's constant and repeated reiki healing touch, especially when my ministering with the dying and grieving has pushed me to my emotional limits, has enabled me not only to survive but to thrive as a "wounded healer." Holding someone in local "hands-on" reiki, or non-local "distant" reiki, provides a safe container or spiritual environment for the healing of grief, loss, and trauma. Bruce's reiki is a sacrament of divine healing in my life – a visible sign of my ultimate connectedness with God.

Professional and non-professional caregivers need to attend to their own spiritual and emotional well-being, especially as it relates to relational pain, grief, loss, and trauma. When we honor our own healing process, we can more creatively and appropriately respond to the pain of others. Every professional caregiver – minister, physician, nurse, psychotherapist – needs a circle of healing companions who support their personal growth, healing, and ministry. The same need for support applies to family members and friends who are called upon to take the final journey with a spouse, parent, child, or companion. Healing is always communal as well as individual in nature. Our own healing and our ability to be healing partners with others are intimately connected.

While we recognize that The Palisades Community Church is unusual in its openness to reiki and other forms of spiritual formation and healing touch, there is growing movement among churches to join pastoral care, prayer, touch, and contemplation. We believe that the practice of reiki healing touch – along with worship, spiritual formation, service, and outreach – awakens a congregation to the surprising possibilities of God's own healing touch in our lives. In a time when many mainstream and progressive churches are struggling to find spiritual practices that are congruent with their theological perspective, the use of reiki healing touch along with contemplative practices, such as centering prayer and healing imagination, affirm the belief that God's universal inspiration and goal of wholeness is the foundation for Christianity and every other authentic quest for transformation.

6

PRACTICES FOR THE WAY

You are the light of the world. A city on a hill cannot be hid... let your light shine before others, so that they may see your good works and give glory to your [Parent] in heaven.

Matthew 5:14, 16

[D]o you not know that your body is a temple of the Holy Spirit within you, which you have from God, and that you are not your own. For you were bought with a price; therefore glorify God in your body.

1 Corinthians 6:19–20

Jesus' first followers called themselves people of the Way. They believed that the early Christian affirmation, Jesus Christ is "the way, the truth, and the life" called them to a lifelong spiritual journey, whose goal was to embody the mind and spirit of Christ.

Reiki is also an all-encompassing way of life, whose primary purpose is to bring healing to ourselves and to the planet. As Christians, we claim this ministry in the spirit of Christ the Healer, "in whom we live, move, and have our being." Reiki practitioners are people of the light, who seek to embody the energy of love in everything we do – from washing dishes and preparing lunches for school-age children, to watering the garden or visiting shut-ins, to hugging a grandchild or peacefully resolving a marital or work-related conflict. To live by the path of reiki is to affirm the biblical insights that we are the light of the world; our bodies are a temple of the Holy Spirit; and that wherever we are, we can let the light of God shine.

From the beginning, Mikao Usui infused the practice of reiki with spiritual principles that shape our attitudes toward life. Along with the reiki attunements and hand positions, the reiki lifestyle inspires us to a life of integrity and love, which opens wide the channels of God's healing energy. The reiki principles were life-transforming for Usui's first reiki students in the slums of Kyoto, and they can positively shape our lives today.

Just for today, do not worry.
Just for today, do not be angry.
Honor your teachers, your parents, your
neighbors, your friends.
Give thanks for all living things.
Earn your living honestly.

Those of us who seek to practice reiki in light of our pilgrimage as followers of Christ's way are reminded of Jesus' words to his first disciples.

Therefore I tell you, do not worry about your
life, what you will eat or what you will drink,
or about your body, what you will wear. Is not

*life more than food, and the body more than
clothing? Look at the birds of the air; they neither
sow nor reap nor gather into barns, and yet your
heavenly [Parent] feeds them... And can any of
you by worrying add a single hour to the span of
your life? And why do you worry about clothing.
Consider the lilies of the field, how they grow;
they neither toil nor spin, yet I tell you, even
Solomon in all his glory was not clothed like of
these. But if God so clothes the grass of the field,
which is alive today and tomorrow is thrown in
the oven, will he not much more clothe you – you
of little faith?... But strive first for the kingdom
of God and [God's] righteousness, and all these
things will be given to you as well.*

Matthew 6:25–30, 33

In the spirit of Christ's counsel, reiki is a way of life grounded
in an awareness of God's universal energy of light and love
in all things. This graceful and abundant energy of life flows
through us and provides for our deepest needs. We do not have
to worry about tomorrow because we are always connected to
a bountiful source of transformation, insight, and love.

Reiki healing does not require a particular talent or
exalted state of mind, but simply an awareness of God's
presence and a willingness to be a channel of blessing to
others. Because God's healing power is all-pervasive, we
can claim our role as healers. God's light flows through us
to bring healing light to others.

Although the divine light flows and the glow of divine
healing illumines all things, we can choose consciously to
open ourselves more fully to being Christ's healing partners.

We can choose to become light-bearers and pioneers on the healing way. We can awaken more fully to this light by following certain practices and attitudes of mind. These practices enable us to channel God's grace with greater clarity, integrity, purpose, and love.

PRACTICES FOR THE HEALING WAY

The healing way embraces the conscious integration of the inner and outer journey through spiritual practices, the healing of the mind, and loving action. As we discover our own spiritual rhythm, many of these practices can gently filter through our everyday lives, bringing a greater sense of peace and well-being to every situation. We will discover the forces of healing in the mundane as well as dramatic moments of life.

The healing affirmation

Jesus' ministry invited persons to see themselves from a new perspective. The healing of the mind that arose from awakening to God's vision for their lives enabled tax collectors to see themselves as spiritual leaders, prostitutes to envisage themselves as lovers, women to claim their role as disciples and ministers, lepers to see the beauty beyond their scars, persons with disabilities to stand up on the inside and then on the outside, and cowards to become fearless martyrs. Jesus recognized that our thought patterns profoundly shape our vision of reality and our interpretation of the events of our lives. Jesus knew that faith lives by its affirmations rather than by its negations. As Paul was to proclaim a few decades after the Resurrection, "Do not be conformed to the world, but be transformed by the renewing of your minds" (Romans 12:2).

In reality, spiritual affirmations are a form of theology in action. The process of Christian spiritual formation involves claiming the basic Christian affirmations of faith and then grounding them in everyday life by living with them moment by moment through mindful repetition. Our affirmations enable us to move from our intellect to our emotions and actions as we live out of the awareness that "God is my (our) creator," "God loves me (us)," "Christ is alive in my (our) life," "I (we) have eternal life," "God is my (our) companion wherever I (we) go."

Healing affirmations awaken us to our divine beauty and power by cleansing the mind of self-imposed or socially imposed limitations, negative self-talk, and low self-esteem. They tell us who we really are – God's beloved sons and daughters who possess more power than we can imagine. Implicit in Jesus' healing encounters was a reversal of the question he asked his disciples: "Who do you say that I am?" To those who sought wholeness, he asks "Who do you say that *you* are? Are *you* worthy of healing? Can *you* trust God enough to risk embarrassment? Can *you* see yourself as a fearless and beloved daughter or son of God?"

When they are regularly repeated, healing affirmations transform not only our conscious but our unconscious mind. They truly enable us to see the world and our own lives with the eyes of Christ. They illumine and transform our minds, and open our lives to a greater influx of divine power. While there are countless affirmations to choose from, I invite you to explore the following affirmations of healing faith. These scripturally based affirmations remind us that we are embodiments of God's creative light and that we can share that light with others.[1]

- Universal energy flows through me, giving me strength and health.
- The energy of love flows through me and enables me to love others.
- God's healing light shines in and through me.
- I am the light of the world. My shining light brings healing to all I meet.
- I bring healing to everyone I touch.
- I use my hands solely for healing and blessing.
- My body is a temple of God.
- My mind is constantly enlightened by the light of Christ.
- God's light brings me health and wholeness.
- I share God's abundant light and love with everyone I meet.
- God's wisdom guides me in every situation.
- God's light constantly energizes and inspires me.
- Divine light guides me through life's darkness.
- In God's light, I find the answer I need in every situation.
- I am walking in the light wherever I go. I can never be lost or alone.
- I can do all things with Christ who strengthens me.
- My God shall supply all my needs.
- Nothing can separate me from the love of God in Christ Jesus.

We are also healed by study and education. As Christians who follow the reiki way, we are called to ground ourselves in scripture, devotional reading, theological reflection, and to explore books on holistic healing and the relationship between spirituality and health.

Those who desire to participate in a community of learning might find a reading group on spirituality and health helpful, as well as regular participation in workshops, retreats, and conferences. New ideas bring greater stature and invite us to alternative approaches to the ministry of healing. As children of the holy adventure, we affirm that there is always more light to shine on our healing path.

The circle of silence and meditation

A dear friend and mother of two pre-teen children recently expressed the unusual joy she felt when her husband and family left town for an overnight holiday. For nearly 24 hours, she did not utter a word. Though our friend is a loving spouse and mother, she needed a break to renew her spirit. She needed to find a "still point" in her quotidian world of moment-by-moment crises and demands.

On a number of occasions, Jesus also needed to surround himself with silence and solitude. As Matthew's gospel notes, following the death of John the Baptist,

> Jesus...withdrew from [Nazareth] in a boat to a deserted place by himself. But when the crowds heard it, they followed him on foot from the towns. When he went ashore, he saw a great crowd; and he had compassion for them and cured their sick.
>
> Matthew 14:13–14

We can all relate to Jesus' experience. We, too, need to withdraw from the demands of everyday life. We need to immerse ourselves in the depths of the Spirit. But often, as soon as we take time out for prayer or holy reading, we get interrupted by the phone ringing, a child banging the door, or a neglected task pressing in on our thoughts. Like Jesus, we need a circle of silence to renew our spirits and to give us guidance for the challenges ahead. For persons who give much of themselves as healing agents in the world, silence is an important resource for sustaining the compassion necessary to feed the multitudes that seek our care.

The circle of silence can be nurtured in the most simple of ways. With the Quakers, we can simply find a place to be still and know that God is present. In silence, we can mindfully open ourselves to the "inner light of Christ" that is the deepest reality of ourselves and all things. From that inner light, we see the light of God in others and, like the Quakers, we are inspired to work for peace and justice. Awakened to the omnipresent light of God, we become citizens of a world without strangers or enemies.

A circle of meditative focus is also a way of seeing more deeply into reality. We can cultivate the silence of our eyes by prayerful appreciation of something as simple as the beauty of the lilies of the field, the birds of the air, a flying insect, the monarch butterfly, a friend's freckled face, or even the hairs on our arm. If, as Meister Eckhardt believed, all things are words of God, then each creature is a mirror of the eternal. Through meditative prayer, we let God's light speak forth in the silence that fills our senses with radical amazement.

Many modern Christians have integrated "centering prayer" into their other spiritual disciplines. Grounded in the mysticism of the English spiritual classic *The Cloud of Unknowing*, centering prayer involves letting God's light shine in our lives by using a single prayer word or phrase as our spiritual focus. Centering prayer involves the following simple steps.

1. Find a quiet, comfortable place, where you can close your eyes and rest in God's spirit.
2. Enter into a moment of prayer.
3. Focus on a meaningful word, such as "love," "light," "healing," "Jesus," "Spirit," "healing."
4. Take a gentle attitude toward interruptions and random thoughts. Simply return to the focus word without judgment.
5. Conclude with a prayer of thanksgiving after 15–20 minutes.

While traditional meditative prayer is silent, some people may feel more comfortable chanting a word or a song out loud, singing a meditative chant such as those popularized by the Taizé community in France, or listening to music especially designed for meditation. Others may choose to focus on a favorite hymn, contemporary praise song, or gospel melody while preparing food or working in the garden.

In the circle of meditative focus, the whispered word of God touches our hearts and the light within guides us toward the next steps of our journey. In meditative prayer, we discover the peace that passes all understanding, even on the most demanding days. A meditative spirit enables us, as followers of the reiki way, to discern the deepest needs of those who seek our healing touch.

Walking in the light

A spiritual exercise Bruce particularly enjoys involves aerobic prayer walking. As he walks, he images breathing in the light of God. Breathing deeply, he experiences God's light healing and illuminating his mind; forehead; lips; throat; heart and lungs; stomach, intestines, and bowel; hips, legs, and feet. After he has reached his feet, Bruce focuses on the presence of God's light moving back up his body in reverse order. His areas of focus are similar to those energy centers identified as the *chakras* in Buddhist and Hindu thought, and the energy points of traditional Chinese medicine. Walking in the light energizes, balances, and affirms the body as a temple of God's spirit.

Kate integrates stretching, breathing, and chanting with her spiritual devotions. The growing interest in body prayer reminds us that our bodies are temples of God and that moving with the spirit grounds and enlivens the cells of our bodies as well as our spiritual energy fields. Other Christians have found that the practice of yoga enables them to experience greater spiritual and mental focus, as well as greater physical energy and well-being.

While there are many forms of exercise that are compatible with the reiki walk, the key element is the interplay of joy and discipline. In the film *Chariots of Fire*, Olympic runner Eric Liddel affirms that "God made me fast, and when I run I can feel God's pleasure." As you look at your life, what form of exercise or physical discipline truly "moves" you in the spirit – walking, dancing, stretching, swimming, jogging, T'ai Chi, Qi Gong, yoga? Take time to discern the physical activity that brings you joy and then make it a regular part of your spiritual life by joining it with a meditative focus. As Christians, we can faithfully embrace practices as diverse as yoga and T'ai Chi because God is the source of all truth and healing.

Self-care
Although God calls us to love our neighbors as we love ourselves, many caregivers fail to love themselves, especially in terms of their relationships, self-care, and bodily affirmation.

Many caregivers give reiki treatments and pray for others, but seldom receive the same loving touch from others. We also forget that we need healing partners in order to nurture our own spiritual and physical well-being and to support our ministry of wholeness and healing. Our healing partners constitute our own healing circle through their prayers, professional and spiritual support, and reiki treatments. Developing a community of healing partners with whom you regularly give and receive healing touch is a blessing that will transform your life and empower your own gifts of healing.

However, our wholeness still depends on our own daily self-care. Self-reiki is an essential aspect of the reiki path. Although divine energy flows through us as we give others reiki treatments, we need to be intentional about our own self-care beyond the natural reiki "flow through" effect.

We can enhance our own well-being by giving ourselves daily reiki treatments. Whether we take five or 15 minutes, we will honor and replenish our bodies by this simple act of self-affirmation.

Self-reiki is simple and easy to do. Beginning by placing your hands on the top of your head. Then place them on your forehead, eyes, throat, heart, stomach, and pubic area. Let God's light flow into your whole being, bringing healing to every thought, emotion, action, and cell. You may choose to envisage God's light flowing into your body from the top of your head, as a point of focus during your self-reiki treatments.

A second way to care for yourself through reiki is to "send" yourself energy just as you would send reiki to someone else, using guided imagery and the level two "long-distance" reiki symbols. In this form of petitionary prayer, you can apply reiki to your back and feet, and to other hard to reach places, as well as surround yourself with divine healing energy.

The practice of reiki complements virtually every healing path. As part of your own self-healing, don't hesitate to explore other healing arts such as massage, healing and therapeutic touch, shiatsu, and polarity therapy. Each of these healing paths is a gift of God, which addresses in its own unique way our healing and wholeness.

The healing imagination

There is a long tradition of the using the imagination as a means to more deeply understand scripture. Jesus told parables to transform people's images of God and human existence. Ignatius of Loyola developed imaginative spiritual exercises to enable people to experience the scriptures through all their senses. Today, many spiritual guides and healers use imaginative prayers to promote the healing process and to awaken untapped spiritual insights.

Our imagination is a powerful tool for healing body, mind, and spirit.[2] We invite you to experience a healing meditation based on John 15:1–11: Jesus' image of the vine and branches.

> Take a moment to be still, letting go of the burdens of the day. Find your center in God's light through some relaxed deep breathing, or whatever works best for you.
>
> Quietly read the passage from John's gospel.
>
> As you reflect on the scripture passage, continue to breathe gently and calmly, as you envisage a lovely, abundantly verdant vine growing on an arbor. What kind of vine is it? See the fruit nestled

heavily amidst the leaves. Sense and absorb the vital fecundity of the vine.

Now imagine yourself as one of the branches on the vine. What is it like to be attached to the vine? Experience the life of the vine flowing through you. Are you open or closed to the energy of the vine? Whether open or closed, let the growing energy flow into you, bringing you life and healing.

What type of "fruit" is growing from your life in terms of your gifts and talents? How does your fruitfulness bring joy and health to others?

Now look around. See the other branches. Experience your connection with them. Do you recognize any of the branches? Can you see any friends or family among them? How does your fruitfulness contribute to their growth? In what ways are you receiving nurture and support from the other branches?

Take a moment to experience the vine as a whole. Feel your connection with the totality and the divine life that flows through the vine. Soak in the healing energy that flows from the vine.

Conclude with a prayer of thanksgiving for the vine, your fruitfulness, and the fruitfulness of your companions on the vine.

Healing visualizations are profoundly personal in nature. Feel free to adapt this imaginative meditation to your own needs. The important thing is to allow your imagination to lead you to unexpected places in the divine journey you share with all things.

Using healing imagination can give you greater insight into scripture as well as into your own life. A simple meditation on the healing of Peter's mother-in-law can awaken us to the ordinary healings in our lives. According to the story,

> *After leaving the synagogue [Jesus] entered Simon's house. Now Simon's mother-in-law was suffering from a high fever, and they asked about her. Then he stood over her and rebuked the fever, and it left her. Immediately she got up and began to serve them.*
>
> Luke 4:38–39

An imaginative meditation based on this brief and apparently ordinary account in the life of Jesus and his friends might inspire the following reflections.

Read the scripture through twice, taking a few minutes to let it soak in as you gently breathe in and out the healing presence of God.

Imagine the following situation. You are having company over for dinner. Because your guests are special to you, you want to make the dinner something extraordinary. Who would you like to invite? (Visualize each one.) What would you like to serve them? What extra touches will you add to the meal and to the entertaining? Imagine the joy of the evening ahead.

However, in the course of your preparations, you become ill and have to go to bed. What are your emotions as you ponder canceling the dinner?

As you look at your life today, what are you worried about missing due to some personal issue? What issue is troubling you?

As you convalesce in your room, Jesus enters and sits at the foot of your bed. He asks, "How can I help you?" How do you respond to him?

After a few minutes, Jesus simply announces that you are well, that the illness is gone. How do you feel?

What do you do now that you are well? What things in your life need your care now that God has touched your life?

Conclude your time of imaginative prayer in gratitude for God's healing presence in your life.

Agnes Sanford used imaginative meditations to facilitate the healing of children as well as adults. She believed that creative imagination can be a factor in accelerating the healing process for oneself and others. In ministering to a child with a leaky heart, Sanford invited the young child to play a spiritual game with her.

Pretend you're a big guy going to high school and on the football squad. Shut your eyes and see yourself holding the ball and running ahead of all the other fellows. "Look at that guy," the other kids will say. "Just look at him run! I bet he's got a strong heart!" Then, you say, "Thank you, God, because that's the way it's going to be."[3]

Through the interplay of imagination and medical care, this boy's heart was healed and he returned to normal activities. Methodist healers Ambrose and Olga Worrall concur with Agnes Sanford's emphasis on the importance of a healing imagination in opening the flow of divine energy, both in the one who channels divine healing and in the one who receives it. "In spiritual healing you do visualize. You are holding a thought for a person. You are seeing that particular organ restored to perfection."[4]

Today, countless people put their faith into action as they visualize healing light permeating their bodies during chemotherapy treatments, or see themselves as whole and healthy following surgery. Through healing imagination, they have discovered that all things are possible for those who put their faith in divine possibility.

Holy reading

Throughout the centuries, Christians have experienced scripture intuitively as well as analytically. Inspired by the Spirit, scripture is always intimate and personal. In letting the Spirit speak the *healing word* through the words of scripture, new insights emerge and unexpected spiritual guidance bursts forth.

The practice of holy reading, or *lectio divina* (a prayerful form of listening to the voice of God) can change your life and enlarge your vision of reality. Lectio divina involves the following steps.

1. Slowly read or listen to the scripture twice without analyzing it.
2. Let the words soak in meditatively for several minutes.
3. Ask yourself what word or phrase reaches out and "grabs you"? What part of the scripture addresses you personally today?
4. Ask yourself what its meaning is for you today?
5. Let the word or phrase rise meditatively over and over in your mind as you attend to its deeper spiritual meaning for you.
6. Ask yourself if the scripture inspires you to any particular action?
7. Conclude with a moment of prayerful openness asking that God continue to illumine your life with God's holy word.

Holy reading enables us to escape the current biblical culture wars as we hear the healing word that gives life and health to the words of scripture. Any passage can be used for holy reading. Some examples are
• the creation story (Genesis 1)
• the prologue of John's gospel (John 1:1–14)
• the man at the pool (John 5:1–14)
• the healing of Jairus' daughter (Mark 5:21–24, 35–43)
• the healing of ten persons with leprosy (Luke 17:11–19).

Holy reading can be joined with healing imagination. Such imaginative prayers can be both humorous and insightful. For example, after reflecting on the healing of Jairus' daughter, you might imaginatively put yourself in her place.

Read the following words of scripture.

> *[Jesus] took her by the hand and said to her,*
> *"Talitha cum," which means, "Little girl, get up!"*
> *And immediately the girl got up and began to*
> *walk about. (She was twelve years of age.) At this*
> *they were overcome with amazement. He strictly*
> *ordered them that no one should know about*
> *this, and then told them to give her something*
> *to eat.*
>
> Mark 5:41–43

As you reflect on this picture from life, imagine yourself in a deep sleep. In this deep sleep, what are you experiencing? Do you have any awareness of the "outside" world? Do you hear voices or feel the presence of your parents or others?

In the midst of your deep sleep, you feel someone touch you and you hear the words, "Get up."

How do you feel when you hear these words? What it is like to rouse from this deep slumber?

Who do you see when you open your eyes? What are their reactions to your awakening?

As you stretch, you hear the Healer give the command, "Give this child something to eat." What do you request from your parents? What do you really want to eat today?

As you sit with your parents and other companions, imagine yourself eating this special food.

Conclude by savoring the meal with thanksgiving for the gift of life and the love of Christ.

When Bruce first attempted this healing visualization in a group setting at Ghost Ranch Conference Center in New Mexico, the initial responses were punctuated with laughter and memories. Participants spoke of choosing "grandma's risotto," "grandmother's matzo ball soup," "chocolate ice cream," and "pizza." Abandoning all political correctness, Bruce mentioned "filet mignon." Soon the conversation moved from our favorite meals to what truly feeds us in life, the persons we want to be at supper with us, and our experiences of intimacy with God and others.

Eating with gratitude

At every meal, we are connected with countless others whose care and hard work make it possible for us to gather around the table. In the ecology of life, each meal connects us with farmers, packers, processors, teamsters, stockers, clerks, and many others. Our eating calls us to reflection and gratitude not just for the "hands that made it," but also for those who share table with us and those who are influenced by our eating habits.

Jesus enjoyed a good meal so much that he was accused of being a "glutton and winebibber" by his detractors. Jesus' table fellowship nurtured spirits as well as bodies, as he celebrated the inclusion of outcasts, sinners, and forgotten women. Everyone belongs at the table of God, regardless of gender, wealth, ethnicity, moral purity, or spiritual evolution.

Unlike many other religious traditions, Christianity has never focused on particular dietary restrictions. In part, this relaxed approach to food was the result of the need to welcome non-Jews to the people of the Way. Though we suspect that the early Christian leaders lived according to the Jewish dietary laws, they also recognized that God's grace did not demand any special approach to food. As the apostle Paul counseled to the Christians at Corinth, "All things are lawful for me" [even food sacrificed to pagan idols]. "But not all things are beneficial... I will not be dominated by anything" (1 Corinthians 6:12). Our diets must reflect the interplay of gratitude, enjoyment, and care. Here are some suggestions for "meals that heal."

See your meals in terms of "soul food" rather than "fast food." Take time to prepare your food with love and thanks. You may choose to reiki your food as a means of consecrating both the food and those who gather at the table. When you are eating, take time to savor each morsel. Truly taste what you are eating. Let your eating be a call to prayer and relationship. Share meals, as you are able, with beloved friends and family. Let your meals be sacraments, mediating God's abundant life to you.

Pray for your table partners. As you prepare your meal, prayerfully visualize each of your table partners. Image God's light shining on them. Image the food they will eat truly nourishing their bodies, minds, and spirits. Surround the food and your friends with reiki healing energy.

Eat gently and lovingly. While there is no one particular diet for Christians of the reiki way, we suggest a diet that is rich in nourishing food, rather than processed food. Discover the food that brings you joy and that energizes your body, mind, and spirit. For some, this will lead to a vegetarian or vegan diet, for others to a diet that includes some meat along with generous helpings of fruit and vegetables. Don't forget, in the course of the day, to let the waters of life flow through you by drinking several glasses of water each day.

Eat justly. We are counseled to "live simply, so others may simply live." In the northern hemisphere, our over-consumption is connected to political policies that lead to starvation in developing countries. The healthiest diets, rich in fruits, vegetables, and unprocessed foods are, not surprisingly, the diets that are the most environmentally friendly. While one need not feel guilty after indulging in an occasional cheeseburger or filet mignon, it is important to see the connection between obesity in the northern hemisphere and scarcity in other countries.

In order to be in solidarity with those who hunger, as well as to cleanse your body, you may choose an occasional "fast" from solid food, after consulting with your health care giver. Fasting is a discipline that invites us to recognize that our wholeness and health is found in our relationship with God and our neighbors, and not in our economic well-being or list of possessions.

The healing power of community

Relationship is at the heart of reality. The energy of love joins mind, body, and spirit; God and humankind; humans and the non-human world; and humans with one another. The apostle Paul reminded the divided community of Corinth of its deepest identity.

> *For just as the body is one and has many members, and all the members of the body, though many, are one body, so it is with Christ...*

If one member suffers, all suffer together with it;
if one member is honored, all rejoice together
with it. Now you are the body of Christ and
individually members of it.

1 Corinthians 12:12, 26–27

Reiki affirms the importance of healing relationships. The hands with which we touch others unite us with them in ways that bring healing and wholeness. As we share reiki with others, the energy of creation is magnified in our own lives. The energy that flows to others must first flow through us, cleansing and enhancing our own energy centers. The reiki path often includes the joy of sending reiki, as a form of intercessory prayer, to several people on a daily basis with the awareness that we are also receiving distant reiki from other friends and associates.

Ultimately, the dynamic circle of love embraces both giving and receiving. As we mediate healing to others through reiki, we are invited to receive God's healing touch from others. We block the flow of divine energy whenever we refuse either to give or to receive the love that flows freely and gracefully through all things. Medical studies report that persons who are active in their church's circle of care live longer, cope more effectively with crises, and have fewer incidents of certain illnesses. Connected to the vine – which includes not only the spirit of Christ, but also our fellow "vine-mates" – we bear healthy and vital fruit.

Wholeness includes the gift of healthy friendships. In the Celtic tradition, every pilgrim hoped to have an *anam cara*, or soul friend, with whom to share their spiritual journey. At their best, one's anam cara – a spouse, a spiritual guide, a close male or female friend – holds the mirror of divinity before us and enables us to see our true reflection.

In the practice of reiki, we also need a small group of healing friends who will support our own healing ministry and remind us of God's presence in our lives. Mutual account-ability, which is often characteristic of healing friendships, helps us to safely explore new dimensions of healing and spiritual growth. In healthy relationships and communi-ties, we learn the meaning of interdependence, in which self-affirmation is joined with the affirmation of others, and self-giving emerges from strong personal centeredness and integrity. In sharing the dynamics of another's growth, we discover our own gifts and talents for healing.

The following meditation on the body of Christ provides an inspirational glimpse into the meaning of community.

> Be still in prayerful openness. Lie down or sit comfortably. Let the peace of Christ surround and permeate you. Imagine a healthy and whole body.

> What does it look like? What are its unique gifts? Notice that the body is not homogenous or uniform but has many unique organs and parts, each with its own beauty and purpose.

> What part of the body are you? Visualize your particular part of the body. What is its unique gift to the body? How are you currently using your unique gifts?

> As you look around the body, you notice that you are not alone, but are surrounded by many other

organs and systems. How do these systems support your growth and empowerment? Which persons in the body are most supportive to you? What are the gifts they bring to you? Are you willing to receive them? Visualize each of your companions in the body, gratefully acknowledging God's presence in your life as mediated through these other parts of the body. What gifts are you currently giving to your companions? What, if anything, is keeping you from sharing your gifts with your friends in the body?

Conclude your imaginative prayer with a time of thanksgiving for the divine gifts of friendship and support.

Sacred service

The biblical creation stories affirm that we exist in an intricate web of relationships, in which personal and global healing and wholeness are united. In the circle of life, our service to others contributes to our own well-being. Medical studies note the "helper's high," in which persons who are active in service and volunteer work experience greater levels of energy, hope, and self-esteem than do non-volunteers. One study, humorously described as the "Mother Teresa Effect," found that even watching videos of Mother Teresa may enhance immune system functioning. Our vitality and life-force is heightened when we touch one another with healing hands and with acts of service. In the spirit of God's promise to Abraham and Sarah, we are "blessed to be a blessing."

Loving service is at the heart of reiki. As the energy of love flows through us, we discover that perceived boundaries between self and other disappear. Reiki helps us to understand that the universe is a hologram in which each part is interdependently related to the others, both locally and cosmically. The reality of universal energy which reiki honors and which we, as Christians, call the Spirit of Christ, is the deepest reality of all things.

Service enlarges our soul in such a way that we experience the well-being of others as essential to our own well-being. Service also connects us with the healing Spirit of Christ residing in all things. Aligned with the Spirit of Christ, our lives and actions become our gifts to God. We believe that our loving actions actually have an impact on God. To do something beautiful for God is our greatest gift to the universe. Jesus affirmed the relationship between serving our neighbor and serving God in his parable of the Last Judgment.

> Then the king will say to those at his right hand, "Come you that are blessed by my [Parent], inherit the kingdom prepared for you from the foundation of the world; for I was hungry and you gave me some food, I was thirsty and you gave me something to drink, I was a stranger and you welcomed me, I was naked and you gave me clothing, I was sick and you took care of me, I was in prison and you visited me." Then the righteous will answer him, "Lord, when was it that we saw you hungry and gave you food, or thirsty and gave you something to drink? And when was it that we saw you a stranger and welcomed you, or naked and gave you clothing? And when was it that we saw you sick or in prison and visited you?" And the king will

answer them, "Truly I tell you, just as you did it
to one of the least of these who are members of
my family, you did it to me."
Matthew 25:34–40

The healing touch of reiki unites us in companionship with all creatures. As "little Christs," we channel divine energy in every encounter. Our healing hands and hearts join us with the sea of healing energy that gives life and light to all creation.

THE HEALING VISION

What has come into being…was life, and the life
was the light of all people… The true light, which
enlightens everyone, was coming into the world.
John 1:3–4, 9

The path of Christian reiki begins and ends with the celebration of God's healing light as revealed in the Healer from Nazareth. God's light flows through our minds, bodies, and spirits. The divine light bursts forth from within each cell and guides our planetary journey. The light that became embodied in Jesus of Nazareth shines through every healing path and radiates through the healing touch of reiki. Gentle and quiet in nature, reiki enables ordinary people to do extraordinary things – to bring light and healing to their world. As we go forth joining the paths of the healer Jesus and reiki healing touch, let us live by the energetic love that will be our companion in unexpected adventures of health, wholeness, and reconciliation.

We conclude with a meditative vision that joins healing of persons with healing of the planet.

In a moment of quiet, relax and breathe in the peace of God which is our deepest reality. Let the breath flow in and out in gratitude for the gift of life and love, for the blessings of this lifetime.

In the quiet, imagine a point of light deep in your own self, the place where your light and Christ's light meet. This light is as old as the big bang, and as timeless as the wisdom of God that brought all things into being. This light joins you with all the other lights of creation.

As you breathe in and out, let the light shine within you. With each breath, listen to God's whispering words of affirmation: "I am the light of the world." Let the breath of light flow from you. Let it flow into your spouse, your children, a special friend, a stranger, an enemy... See the light emerging from each one. With each breath, let God whisper as you acknowledge each one's beauty and wonder: "You are the light of the world." Look beyond your immediate world. Look deeply into mountains, oceans, city streets, rushing rivers. Let the light of Christ flow forth from everything you see.

As the light shines through you, experience it flowing from your hands, your thoughts, and your emotions. See it touching another, filling them with health, wholeness, and love. See the light joining you with all things.

Let that inner light of Christ radiate from your heart and hands through your family, your community, your nation, the whole earth, the solar system, the galaxy, the universe.

Again, let the light shine deep within you. It is the light of Christ, the light embodied in Jesus, the light of healing. Let your healing light shine. Embrace the energy of love that heals yourself and the universe. Amen.

Endnotes

Prologue

[1] Harold Keonig, *Is Religion Good for Your Health?* (New York: Haworth, 1997) and *The Healing Power of Faith* (New York: Simon and Schuster, 1999).

[2] Larry Dossey, *Prayer Is Good Medicine* (San Francisco: HarperSanFrancisco, 1996) and *Healing Words* (San Francisco: HarperSanFrancisco, 1993).

[3] Kenneth Pelletier, *The Best Alternative Medicine* (New York: Simon and Schuster, 2000).

[4] Herbert Benson, *Timeless Healing* (New York: Scribner's, 1996).

[5] See Dolores Krieger, *Therapeutic Touch* (Englewood Cliffs, NJ: Prentice-Hall, 1979); Linda Smith, *Called into Healing* (Arvada, CO: HTSM Press, 2000); *Healing Touch: A Guide for Practitioners* (Albany, NY: Delmar, 2002); Rochelle Graham, Flora Litt, Wayne Irwin, *Healing from the Heart* (Kelowna, BC: Wood Lake Books, 1998).

Chapter One

[1] Frank Arjava Petter, *Reiki Fire* (Twin Lakes, WI: Lotus Light, 1997) and *Reiki: The Legacy of Dr. Usui* (Twin Lakes, WI: Lotus Light, 1999). Petter's thesis is that Usui was born and died as a committed Buddhist. Petter suggests that the insertion of Christian elements in the reiki story was intended to make reiki more accessible to the Western world following World War II. Given the antagonism against Japanese culture, reiki might not initially have found a following in the United States without a more Western veneer. While Petter's work as a historian is modest, we find his basic premise interesting – that Usui was a Buddhist, who never traveled to America nor embraced the Christian faith. Still, beneath the possible inaccuracies of the Westernized reiki story is an important truth – the quest for global healing that goes beyond ethnic and religious distinctions.

[2] One of the clearest expressions of this version of the traditional reiki story is to be found in Helen Haberly, *Reiki: Hawayo Takata's Story* (Garrett Park, MD: Archedigm, 1990), 2–10.

[3] For a discussion of the cultural and spiritual context of the Pentecostal movement, see Harvey Cox, *Fire from Heaven* (New York: DaCapa, 2001).

[4] Agnes Sanford, *The Healing Light* (St. Paul: Macalester Park Publishing, 1972) and Olga and Ambrose Worrall, *The Gift of Healing* (Columbus: Ariel Publishing, 1985).

Chapter Two

[1] Marcus Borg and N. T. Wright, *The Meaning of Jesus: Two Visions* (San Francisco: HarperSanFrancisco, 1999), 66.

[2] Morton Kelsey, *Psychology, Medicine, and Christian Healing* (New York: Harper and Row, 1988), 42–43.

[3] John Dominic Crossan, *Jesus: A Revolutionary Biography* (San Francisco: HarperSanFrancisco, 1994), 70.

[4] Ibid., 82.

[5] Candace Pert, *The Molecules of Emotion* (New York: Scribner, 1997).

[6] Ibid., 130–195.

[7] Larry Dossey, *Healing Words* (San Francisco: HarperSanFrancisco, 1993); Dale Matthews, *The Faith Factor* (New York: Viking, 1998).

Chapter Three

[1] Agnes Sanford, *The Healing Light* (St. Paul, Minnesota: Macalester Park Publishing, 1972), 13.

[2] Ibid., 19, 31.

[3] Ibid., 31.

[4] Larry Dossey, *Healing Words*, 83–84.

Chapter Four

[1] "Order of Service for Healing for Congregational Use," *Book of Worship: United Church of Christ* (New York: Office for Church Life and Leadership, 1986), 318–319.

[2] Ibid., 315–316.

[3] Haberly, *Reiki*, 12.

[4] Ambrose and Olga Worrall, *Explore Your Psychic World* (Columbus: Ariel Press, 1970), 83.

[5] A detailed description of contemporary forms of these ancient practices will be outlined in chapter six.

[6] We will describe the significant role of reiki in pastoral care settings in the next chapter.

[7] Adapted from a quote in Linda L. Smith, *Called into Healing* (Arvada, CO: HTSM Press, 2000), 183.

[8] Gabriele Uhlein, *Meditations with Hildegard of Bingen* (Santa Fe: Bear and Company, 1983), 90.

[9] Gary Gunderson, *Deeply Woven Roots* (Minneapolis: Fortress Press, 1997), 9.

[10] Quoted in Tilda Norberg and Robert Webber, *Stretch Out Your Hand* (Nashville: Upper Room, 1999), 94.

[11] Gary Gunderson, *Deeply Woven Roots,* 6.

[12] For a reflection on the relationship between personal and social wholeness, see Bruce Epperly and Lewis Solomon, *Mending the World: Spiritual Hope for Ourselves and Our Planet* (Philadelphia: Innisfree, 2002).

[13] Haberly, *Reiki,* 8.

[14] Walter Wink, *Engaging the Powers* (Philadelphia: Fortress Press, 1992), 65.

[15] George McLain, *Claiming All Things for God* (Nashville: Abingdon, 1998), 13–14.

[16] Adapted from Bruce Epperly and Anna Rollins, "A Service of Healing and Blessing: Touched by God," in *Creative Transformation* 11:1 (Winter). This service was first conducted at the Kirkridge Retreat and Conference Center, Bangor, Pennsylvania. It was composed as a concluding worship service for a retreat on "The Healings of Jesus and Reiki Healing," led by Bruce Epperly and assisted by Rev. Kate Epperly, D.Min. We dedicate this service to Morton Kelsey who pioneered healing ministries at Kirkridge.

Chapter Six

[1] For a thorough study of the relationship of theology, spiritual formation, and the use of affirmations, see Bruce Epperly, *The Power of Affirmative Faith: A Spirituality of Personal Transformation* (Chalice Press, 2001).

[2] For more detailed healing visualizations, Bruce Epperly, *God's Touch: Faith, Wholeness, and the Healing Miracles of Jesus* (Lousville:Westminster/John Knox, 2001); *The Power of Affirmative Faith*; Bruce Epperly and Lewis Solomon, *Mending the World.*

[3] Agnes Sanford, *The Healing Light,* 28–29.

[4] Ambrose and Olga Worrall, *Explore Your Psychic World* (Columbus: Ariel Press, 1970), 98.

REV. BRUCE G. EPPERLY, PH.D., is a reiki master-teacher, an ordained minister in the United Church of Christ and Disciples of Christ, and the author of 11 books and over 100 articles and reviews. Dr. Epperly has appeared on numerous radio and television programs, including *ABC World News Tonight, NightLine, One on One with John McLaughlin,* and *PBS Evening News.* Bruce is Director of the Alliance for the Renewal of Ministry and Continuing Education, and Associate Professor of Practical Theology at Lancaster Theological Seminary.

REV. KATHERINE GOULD EPPERLY, D.MIN., is a reiki master-teacher and is certified in pastoral psychotherapy, massage therapy, Myers-Briggs Type Indicator, and massage for persons with cancer and chronic illness. Katherine is an ordained minister in the United Church of Christ and Disciples of Christ and is currently co-pastor, with Bruce, at the Disciples United Community Church in Lancaster, Pennsylvania.